A-1-7

Tudor Church Music

TUDOR
CHURCH MUSIC

by

DENIS STEVENS

W. W. Norton & Company, Inc.

NEW YORK

Printed in Great Britain

Contents

grammata sola carent fato, mortemque repellunt.
preterita renovant grammata sola biblis.

HRABANUS MAURUS

Preface

Tudor Church Music means, for the majority of musicians, the motets and Masses of William Byrd, together with his anthems and services and those of his contemporaries. This period in English musical history might more accurately be styled Elizabethan, for the House of Tudor was established nearly a century before Byrd became famous, and its early years saw the encouragement of music and musicians on a scale that was hardly equalled even in the most brilliant years of Henry IV's reign. Unfortunately the masterpieces of Fayrfax, Cornyshe, Ludford and their many colleagues in the Chapel Royal are practically unknown. The Catholic Church has not the slightest use for them in its liturgy, nor has the Anglican Church. At the time of writing there is not a single LP record of a preReformation Mass by an English composer, and if it were not for occasional performances on the BBC Third Programme we should have no idea at all of the immense scope and design, the vast potential soncrity of these grandiloquent works. They rank with the very finest of our architecture, stained glass, and statuary; yet they cannot be simply looked at and thus appreciated. They must be sung by the finest choirs and the most skilled soloists available, just as the symphonic masterpieces of the classical era are performed by the best orchestras. Only then will their message become really apparent, and the austere beauty of their texture become a living part of our musical experience.

I have endeavoured to trace the stylistic changes and developments from 1485 until 1603 with special reference to the liturgical forms used principally by composers of the time. Studies of individual composers may be found in standard reference books, while the music of Byrd and Gibbons has been discussed in detail by E. H. Fellowes in his monographs on these composers. My aim has been to discuss the music rather than the men who wrote it, and to provide a survey of the period as a whole instead of concentrating on either the Henrician or Elizabethan periods. It is to be hoped that the reader will progress from the present study to more detailed works such as Reese's *Music in the Renaissance* and Harrison's *Music in Medieval Britain*; yet the appendix of available editions will, I trust, help to make this study a work of reference and utility. I have to thank all those publishers listed in the appendix for their assistance and co-operation, and I also wish to record my gratitude to Dr. Joseph Kerman and Mr. Gilbert Reaney for their kindness in reading the book in proof.

DENIS STEVENS

Note to the Second Edition

Since writing the Preface to the first edition, I find to my pleasure that the availability of music and recordings of Tudor church music has improved to some extent. Old and inaccurate editions are slowly being replaced by new and better ones, and these changes—as well as additions to the repertory—have been taken into account in the complete revision of the *List of Editions*. I wish to thank all those readers who have suggested improvements and called my attention to new material in a constantly changing field of publication, and I am especially grateful to Mr. Francis Cameron, Mr. Peter H. James, Mr. David Josephson, Mr. E. N. J. Miller, and Mr. John Morehen for their valuable and detailed communications. My plea for more recordings of this splendid music appears to have been heard in certain quarters, and it is now possible to hear two of Taverner's Masses (*The Western Wind* and *Gloria tibi Trinitas*) and one by Fayrfax (*Tecum principium*). The first is available on an Argo disc, the second and third on Musica Sacra label which can be ordered from dealers who specialize in continental imports. All three have been recorded in stereo, and all feature shorter works by the same composers. Two records issued by H.M.V. in conjunction with the first two volumes of 'The Treasury of English Church Music' (Blandford) will also be found extremely valuable in studying the music of this period.

DENIS STEVENS

I

History and Liturgy

The closing years of the centuries-old rule of the House of Plantagenet saw a slow but inexorable decline in the stature of English polyphony. This noble art, which had achieved so wide and so enviable a reputation during the reign of Henry V, suffered a mortal blow in the year 1445, when Leonel Power died in Canterbury. Eight years later the death of John Dunstable closed for ever a glorious chapter in the history of English liturgical music, and the Flemish theorist and composer Johannes Tinctoris, summing up events at the moderately safe distance of twenty years or so, felt bound to admit that the English had fallen from their supreme position as inventors of new techniques in music. In comparison with the Franco-Flemish *avant-garde*, they did no more than 'continue to use one and the same style of composition, which shows a lamentable lack of invention'.[1]

Indeed, the situation was rather akin to that which John Bossewell lamented a century later, when he thrusts before us this rhetorical question and answer: 'But what saie I, Musicke? One of the seven Liberall sciences? It is almost banished this Realme.'[2] Yet the enthusiasm and devotion of a few men precluded its entire banishment, in the fifteenth century as in the sixteenth. The craft, as well as the spirit, of the careful and colourful scribes of the Old Hall and Egerton manuscripts was to live on in those who limned the great choirbooks of Eton, Lambeth and Cambridge. Musicians, no less than scribes, gained new heart and courage when Henry VII, the first monarch of the new Tudor dynasty, was crowned on November 7th, 1485.

Henry, as a Lancastrian, had a weak hereditary claim to the throne, but his marriage to Elizabeth of York did much to reconcile the opposing faction and before long both government and treasury began to flourish. The royal marriage called forth musical

---

[1] Tinctoris, *Proportionale musices (c. 1475)*. From the dedicatory epistle to Ferdinand I.

[2] Bossewell, *Workes of armorie, devyded into three bookes, entituled, the concordes of armorie, the armorie of honour, and coates and creastes*. London, 1572.

tributes from two composers who were later to make their mark as distinguished writers of liturgical polyphony: Thomas Ashwell and Gilbert Banester. The former is credited with a composition, apparently not now extant, beginning with the words 'God save King Harry'.[1] If this work really did exist, Ashwell's Mass of the same title (partially preserved in St. John's College and the University Library, Cambridge) would qualify as the earliest Tudor example of a parody Mass: otherwise it must be dismissed as a musicological mirage.

Banester's motet *O Maria et Elizabeth*[2] is far more tangible, and is still to be seen today in the fine choirbook preserved in the college library at Eton. It contains a prayer which reads 'protege quesumus tibi devotum athletam regem nostrum', and although no name is given by the scribe, there is little doubt as to the identity of the monarch, for Banester died in 1487, only two years after Henry's coronation. The comparatively infrequent use of five-part harmony for full choir seems to give the motet an aura of austere strength and quiet dignity.

One other work deserves to be mentioned in connection with occasional or ceremonial music during Henry VII's reign, and that is the motet *Aeterne laudis lilium* by Robert Fayrfax. Elizabeth of York appears to have commissioned the motet, for her Privy Purse expenses for the year 1502 make mention of a payment to Fayrfax 'for setting an anthem of our Lady and Saint Elizabeth'.[3] The name of the saint—and of the queen—is given great musical prominence towards the end of the work, and may well have been intended as a royal compliment.

Ceremonial music aside, there was much for composers to exercise their minds upon in the widespread and complex Sarum liturgy. Although Salisbury was its

[1] Grattan Flood, *Early Tudor Composers*, p. 58.
[2] *The Eton Choirbook* (ed. F. Ll. Harrison), *Musica Britannica* XI, p. 117.   [3] Flood, *op. cit.*, p. 37.

rightful home, and the eleventh-century Rouen ritual its corner-stone, it came to be regarded as the official liturgy in the greater part of England, even of the British Isles. True enough, there was a Use of Hereford, of Bangor, of York, and of Lincoln (though traces of this last have all but disappeared)—yet they varied only slightly from the main source and fountain-head of their inspiration. The elaborate and imposing ceremonial of High Mass called for music of corresponding dignity and equivalent complexity, while the daily Office (especially Matins and Vespers) was in constant need of solemn settings of antiphons, hymns, responsories, and canticles.

High Mass was celebrated after Terce on Sundays and the principal Feasts, after Sext on weekdays and lesser Feasts, and after None during Advent, Lent and Vigils.[1] The actual time of the day varied, of course, with the time of the year; but it may easily be seen that a composer or singer serving a large ecclesiastical establishment, whether abbey, cathedral or Chapel Royal, could be expected to take his proper part in services at various times of the day. In many cases he would compose the music asked of him by the Precentor, rehearse it with the members of the choir, and sing in it (whilst directing from his stall) during the service.

How he came to compose it is a question which has long interested musicians and scholars, for they realize only too well that the choirbook (with separate voice-parts on adjacent pages) and the part-books which flourished at a later date, represent only the final version of the music. It certainly existed in score before it was copied out according to its component voice-parts, since it is obviously difficult to compose complex polyphony other than in score.[2] Yet scores had little attraction for musicians of the Renaissance. An exactly corresponding situation may be seen in the vocal and instrumental music of the Baroque era: then, as in earlier days, a first violinist or continuo player would set the tempo and change it when necessary. In Tudor times, the choir-master would set the tempo and attend to the details of performance: a score would have been both a luxury and a hindrance.

The Precentor, at the beginning of every week, wrote the names of those entrusted with special duties in the ceremony on a waxed board which was hung up in the chapter-house for all to see. At the end of the week, the wax was smoothed over and inscribed upon once more. This is almost certainly the way in which composers wrote their music; valuable parchment and paper were not wasted in rough drafts, and alterations were easy to make. Architects too used waxed boards for their plans; this explains the lack of detailed plans for buildings erected during the Middle Ages. Instead of blueprints and scores, we have cathedrals and choirbooks.

[1] See also J. D. Chambers, *Divine Worship in England in the Thirteenth and Fourteenth Centuries*, p. 309.
[2] The matter is fully discussed by Edward E. Lowinsky, *On the Use of Scores by Sixteenth-Century Musicians*, in *Journal of the American Musicological Society*, I (1948), p. 17. Comments by Ruth Hannas and a reply by Lowinsky may be seen *ibid.*, II (1949), p. 130.

The entire reign of Henry VII and the greater part of Henry VIII's reign saw no major liturgical changes. Composers were thus able to build up a strong tradition in both form and texture, and it is largely due to this tradition that the salient charac/teristics of English polyphony were preserved, in one way or another, until the very end of the century. In matters of form, the liturgy itself was of prime importance by virtue of its wide and almost uniform currency. Texture, however, was a more vari/able factor, depending for the most part upon the number and type of singers avail/able.[1] Most of the larger abbeys and cathedrals, and not a few collegiate churches of the size of Eton or King's College Cambridge, possessed choirs of twenty or more voices. Even a body of sixteen singers was a useful, sonorous and eminently practical asset to the liturgy, for the fashionable norm in texture was five actual voice/parts. Most of Fayrfax's music is in five parts, and if his motet *O bone Jesu* were still complete it would most certainly be written for this disposition of vocal resources, as in the case of the parody Mass based upon it. A nearly contemporary setting of the same text, however, shows us that the density of texture could be four times as great as that used by Fayrfax. The composer of this setting, which contains acclamations written in as many as nineteen real voice/parts,[2] is the Scottish priest Robert Carver, most of whose music dates from the early sixteenth century (see Ex. 2).

A famous medieval description of the love of part/singing in Wales might easily tempt us to trace an equally strong love of music in certain Tudor monarchs to this very same source. Both Henry VIII and Queen Elizabeth were musically gifted: of the former, Henry Peacham tells us in *The Compleat Gentleman* that he 'could not onely sing his part sure, but of himselfe compose a Service of four, five, and sixe parts; As Erasmus in a certaine Epistle, testifieth of his own knowledge'. Many of Henry VIII's compositions have come down to us, as well as works written in his honour.

The motet *Quam pulchra es*, which is ascribed to Henry in the Baldwin manu/script,[3] shows considerable skill in the manipulation of three voice/parts (two tenors and bass), besides a sure grasp of the intricacies of mensural proportions. A musical cleric who enjoyed preferment as well as protection, thanks to royal interest, was Richard Sampson; and it is by no means surprising to discover him as composer—and perhaps author too—of a long motet in praise of King Henry: *Psallite felices*

---

[1] A large amount of church music was undoubtedly intended for men's voices, the uppermost voice/part suggesting the normal counter/tenor range of today. There was, of course, no such thing as absolute pitch in Tudor times, and it is therefore advisable to work out the compass of each voice/part in a motet or Mass and discover which of the accepted tessiturae it will best fit, before risking violent and possibly unmusical transpositions.

[2] *Robert Carver: Omnia Opera*, vol. 1 (ed. D. W. Stevens), *Corpus Mensurabilis Musicae* 16; also in *Music of Scotland* (ed. K. Elliott), *Musica Britannica*, XV.

[3] British Museum, RM 24 d 2, f.166v.

protecti culmine rose purpuree.[1] A prayer for Henry is to be found in a short motet *Christe Jesu pastor bone*, by John Taverner, who used some of the musical material, parody-wise, in his Mass *Small Devotion.*[2]

An ill-controlled temperament allied with a constant anxiety over the succession caused both the annulment of Henry's marriage with Catherine of Aragon, and the sentence of excommunication pronounced by Pope Clement VII in 1533. How this affected church musicians may be seen by the vast number of ecclesiastical sub-scribers and signatories to the Act of Supremacy passed in June of the following year. In acknowledging Henry as the supreme head of the English Church, the musicians, in company with all the other church dignitaries, helped to create a liturgical *impasse* which was not to be finally disposed of until the Act of Uniformity of 1662, during the reign of Charles II. Shortly after 1535, composers began to experiment with musical settings of Marshall's English version of the Sarum *Horae*; in 1539, the year of the 'Great Bible', Hilsey's *Prymer* succeeded Marshall's. Henry VIII's *Prymer*, published in 1545, led the way to the first Book of Common Prayer ratified in 1549 by the first Act of Uniformity.[3] To add to this confusion over texts to be set to music, there was confusion in the very ranks of musicians themselves, for the dissolution of monasteries and abbey churches between 1535 and 1540 resulted in a widespread redistribution of musical talent throughout the whole of England. There is no doubt that the finest of the musicians were quickly absorbed into the changing framework of the English church, and for many of them the change must have meant a temporary loss of prestige, though not necessarily a loss of salary.

[1] British Museum, Royal 11 E xi, f.3v. This exceptionally beautiful choir-book contains much in the way of pictorial symbolism referring to the Wars of the Roses and the marriage of Henry VIII with Catherine of Aragon.

[2] Motet and Mass are printed on pp. 73 and 169 respectively of *Tudor Church Music*, III. One of the manuscript sources for *Christe Jesu* replaces Henry's name with that of Elizabeth. Mr. Jeremy Noble has suggested 'Thomam cardinalem' as the original of 'regem nunc Henricum'. See also p. 33, fn. 1.

[3] Fascinating and significant links between music and texts are discussed by Frere, *Edwardine Vernacular Services before the First Prayer Book*, in *Alcuin Club Collections*, XXXV (1940), p. 5.

Perhaps the most remarkable feature of Tudor music is the expression of artistic continuity which it can so often reveal to the student and listener. Although not entirely a continuity of idiom, it possesses an underlying mood and feeling which stamps it as English and therefore as insular. The achievements of the most outstanding among Italian and Franco-Flemish composers were known and respected in well-informed English musical circles; but those same circles, Catholic in both outlook and religion, jealously guarded the finer points of style which eventually set them in a class by themselves. An Italian visitor to Henry VIII's court described the singing of the choristers during High Mass as 'more divine than human', and he admitted that the basses (whose range is admirably portrayed by the choice of the word *contrabassi*) 'probably have not their equals in the whole world'.[1]

That account, written in 1515, may profitably be compared with another (this time from the pen of a German visitor) much later in the century. The place was Windsor; the occasion was morning service in St. George's Chapel: 'the music, especially the organ, was exquisitely played, for at times you could hear the sound of cornetts, flutes, then fifes and other instruments; and there was likewise a little boy who sang so sweetly amongst it all, and threw such a charm over the music with his little tongue, that it was really wonderful to listen to him'.[2] Captain Cooke of the Chapel Royal used cornetts to double his singers mainly in order to keep them in tune, for they were sadly out of practice during the Commonwealth. No such discouragement of musical talent can be laid at the door of the Reformation, however, and the continuity of choral excellence which is apparent in the continental tributes just quoted went hand in hand with a similar flow of creative activity.

Composers were not, as a rule, unwilling to set English words to music. They did so as a matter of course in their court-songs, part-songs, and madrigals. Para-liturgical forms including carols for Christmas, Easter, and other feasts had been closely bound up with the vernacular since the middle of the fifteenth century, and it had even become fashionable to mix Latin and English texts. An example of this macaronic procedure as applied to a setting of the canticle *Te Deum* may be seen in the composition by Thomas Packe.[3] An ostensibly normal opening verse, with the cantor's intonation answered by five-part polyphony, is followed immediately by an English gloss: 'We praise the, almighty god; we knowlych the oure mercyfulle lord.' Thereafter odd Latin words appear in the midst of the English text, with the complete phrase 'Te Dominum confitemur' coming round as a chorus at the end of every verse.

---

[1] Sagudino, writing from London to the Signory of Venice in June, 1515. *Calendar of State Papers, Venetian*, II, p. 247.

[2] Jacob Rathgeb, *Kurtze und warhaffte Beschreibung der Badenfahrt* (Tübingen, 1602), quoted by W. B. Rye, *England as seen by Foreigners in the Days of Elizabeth and James the First*. London, 1865.

[3] British Museum, Add. Ms. 5665, f.95v.

The real difficulty about setting texts from the various Prymers was not a religious one, but a musical difficulty born of Cranmerian contortions. It was Cranmer who first confused the musico-liturgical functions of homophony and polyphony; and it is much to the credit of Tudor composers that they extracted themselves so rapidly from the chains he sought to throw about them. The sequences and hymns of the Sarum rite, together with hymns and special prayers set by musicians in conductus style, all fundamentally anticipated Cranmer's precepts for the new style of church music—that is, not 'full of notes [melismatic] but, as near as may be, for every syllable a note'. One might add 'for every two syllables a step', since certain hymns were meant to be sung during procession, and their function was to provide a steady and dignified rhythmic pulse. Cranmer seized this simple and rhythmical style of writing and proceeded to apply it to non-processional activities, to which it was obviously not suited.[1] Since processions came to be frowned upon as superstitious and unnecessary, and the Litany itself was sung in procession only very rarely (as at Rogationtide), it is not surprising that the projected English version of the Sarum *Processionale* came to nothing. Composers did indeed try to simplify their part-writing, and there is no doubt that their efforts had a welcome if astringent effect upon Elizabethan style; but they could no more find true inspiration in an anthem sounding like a slow-motion frottola, than their architectural colleagues could abide a return to quadripartite vaulting after having perfected in stone the miraculous counterpoint of tierceron and lierne.

The Bodleian manuscripts known as the Wanley part-books[2] (after a former owner) exemplify the many different cross-currents of musical thought and texture which existed side by side during the last decade of Henry VIII's reign. But only two out of ten Communion services can be said to follow Cranmer's sober and solemn injunctions; of the remaining eight, four are not unduly florid, while the other four are distinctly so. Two of the florid settings are adaptations, probably by the composer himself, of the Masses *Sine Nomine* and *Small Devotion* by John Taverner, who—however much he may have repented of his 'Popish ditties'—yet found it convenient to retain the music and substitute only a new verbal text.[3] Thus, in spite of recurring objections, the Tudor composers continued in their understandable reluctance to abandon the horizontal aspect of musical texture, and their stubborn attitude bore healthy fruit in later years.

The closely interrelated affairs of church and state gave rise to an increased number

---

[1] His letter to Henry VIII has often been misunderstood and misquoted, but it does seem that the principle 'for every syllable a note' refers also to the canticles, psalms, and sections of the Mass mentioned individually in this letter. The text is reprinted by Fellowes, *English Cathedral Music*, p. 25.

[2] Ms. Mus. Sch. E 420–422. See Frere, *op. cit.*, for partial listing of contents.

[3] The phrase 'Popish ditties' almost certainly refers to his large-scale setting of Marian antiphons, rather than to his Masses.

of prayers for the king, ranging from a simple clause in the 1544 Litany to an elaborate, and possibly eight-part setting of a prayer for Edward VI.[1] Two syllabic and
four-part Litanies appear in the Wanley manuscripts, and they both use, or rather fit
(for the tenor part-book is missing) the plainsong which Cranmer issued with his
Litany. England being then at war with Scotland, and in a state of preparation for
war with France, special prayers are asked for the King's Majesty 'who at this presente
tyme hath taken upon him the great and daungerous affayres of warre'.

When the youthful Edward VI acceded to the throne in 1547, plans were already
in hand to enforce the reading of Epistle and Gospel in English during High Mass.
These plans were ratified in the royal Injunctions, which also expressly forbade processions. Injunctions delivered in the following year to the Dean and Chapter of
Lincoln Cathedral demanded of them that 'they shall from henceforth sing or say no
anthem of our Lady or other Saints, but only of our Lord, and them not in Latin; but
choosing out the best and most sounding to Christian religion they shall turn the same
into English, setting thereunto a plain and distinct note for every syllable one; they
shall sing them and none other'.[2] The anti-Marian feeling was thus gradually in-
tensified; and Tudor composers lost what was perhaps one of their most characteristi-
cally intimate forms of devotion—the motet in honour of the Blessed Virgin.

Early in 1549, Grafton and Whitchurch were busily engaged in printing the First
Book of Common Prayer, which was ordered to be used exclusively in all churches
throughout the land on and after Whitsunday, June 9th. It was not well received by
church dignitaries, most of whom considered that it should undergo further, even
drastic, reform before being wholeheartedly adopted. Composers were therefore still
in an awkward state of not knowing for certain whether the liturgy would survive,
and it is not surprising that they turned their energies to the setting of anthems, such
as those contained in the set of Edwardian part-books, unfortunately no longer

[1] British Museum, Roy. App. 74–76.
[2] Frere and Kennedy, *Visitation Articles and Injunctions of the Period of the Reformation*, II, p. 168.

complete, in the British Museum.[1] Here, as in the Wanley part-books, most of the compositions are anonymous; it is almost as if anonymity in this time of musical experiments were a kind of cloak with which to hide the current utilitarian apparel. The prayer for Edward may well have been written in July or August of 1549, shortly before yet another declaration of war upon the French: 'O lorde Christe Jesu that art kyng in glory and very perfit roote of all our felicity, we sinners do most humbly beseech thy hy majesty to graunt thy noble servant our sovereign lorde King Edward, that he may have thorough thee ovyr all his enemies most ryall victory . . .'

In 1553 Edward died of consumption, and the Reformation which had made such headway under the aegis of the Protector, Somerset, suffered a temporary though violent reverse at the hands of Queen Mary. It was during her reign that Philip of Spain and his court paid a visit to England, and there still exist accurate accounts of the royal meeting at Winchester, where all attended High Mass in the cathedral. Although Antonio de Cabezón, in charge of Philip's musicians, was then at the height of his powers as a composer and organist, it is extremely doubtful whether he had any direct influence on English music of the time. In the first place, the political atmosphere was far too unsettled for any real *rapprochement* between musicians of the English and Spanish chapels. The stern measures adopted by Mary must have done much towards alienating her subjects from the retinue of her guests, and an unpopular and childless marriage did not help matters. In the second place, the music which was published by Henestrosa in 1557 does not show Cabezón in a very favourable light, though it proves that he was a composer of taste and one whose sense of liturgical values was impeccable.[2] But in the field of virtuosity, experiment, and ideas the English organists (whose works have unfortunately not been published in anything like their entirety) are far and away superior to the Spaniard, and it is clear from their highly individual style that they could have learnt little from even the greatest of European keyboard players.

John Barnard, who in 1641 was the first ever to print an anthology of English church music, said that Elizabeth's reign 'brought forth a noble birth, as of all learned men, so of Famous Composers in Church-Musick'. That this is so true is a sign of the more settled and peaceful nature of the times: violent persecution was almost a thing of the past, and Catholic musicians such as Tallis, Byrd and Morley, were able to hold office in the Chapel Royal. The second Prayer Book, with all its vigorous

[1] These three volumes (Roy. App. 74–76) were written towards the very end of Henry VIII's reign, probably in 1546 or 1547. Among the earliest owners were John, Baron Lumley, and Henry Fitzalan, Earl of Arundel.

[2] See Anglés, *La Música en la Corte de Carlos V*, for a complete edition of Henestrosa's *Libro de Cifra Nueva para tecla, harpa y vihuela*, and an account (p. 128) of the journey from Southampton to London via Winchester in 1554, taken from the book by Andrés Muñoz.

denunciation of ceremonial, soon found itself faced with a Latin translation, made by the Cambridge reformer Walter Haddon, and published in 1560. This Latin version of the Prayer Book was intended for use in the Universities and in the colleges of Winchester and Eton, besides royal peculiars like St. George's Chapel, Windsor. Since Latin was allowed as the official language of the services—even of Holy Communion—it was an encouragement to composers to continue in their use of Latin texts.[1] Even Protestant composers used Latin (usually Biblical) texts quite freely, with the result that it is extremely difficult to date a composer's output by the language employed, and even by the style of the music.

It is important that the Reformation in England should be visualized as a gradual change from the Sarum liturgy to the newly-established order of service in the English Church. The overlapping of artistic impulses and the lack of a clearly-defined liturgy over a long period caused a slow change in musical outlook, and that slow change was one of the greatest contributing factors to the continuity of tradition. Latin Masses were underlaid with an English text as early as 1545 by Taverner;[2] on the other hand, new settings of the Mass were composed by Byrd during the last years of Elizabeth's reign, and were (though isolated) eventually published. A very great number of Elizabethan composers have left both Latin and English works, but it is not necessarily true that the former were written at an earlier point in the century than the latter. In the case of Tye, Tallis, John Mundy and Robert Parsons there is every reason to believe that the bulk of their Latin church music was written considerably later than their attempts to abide by Cranmerian formulas. The drive in favour of simplicity achieved a certain amount of purely musical good, however, and melismatic passages declined but did not entirely disappear. The resulting texture was refined without being exquisite, and freely contrapuntal without being dense and impenetrable.

It was in this artistic milieu that Byrd came to learn music, and it was he whose technique and reputation (according to the loquacious commentator of a set of part-books in Christ Church, Oxford) was sufficient to free the English from Cicero's reproach of knowing nothing about music.[3] It was Byrd who set for male voices a short prayer for Queen Elizabeth: 'O Lord, make Thy servant Elizabeth our Queen to rejoice in Thy strength; give her her heart's desire, and deny not the request of her

---

[1] Even as late as the posthumously published *Musica Deo Sacra* of Thomas Tomkins (1668) there are two anthems with alternative Latin texts: *Why art thou so full of heaviness* (*Domine tu eruisti animam*), and *Lord, enter not into judgment* (*Non nobis Domine*).

[2] *Tudor Church Music*, III, pp. 143 and 169.

[3] Christ Church, Mus. Ms. 985, after no. 41: *Cicero ad Atticum lib. 4°. Britannici belli exitus expectatur; etiam iam cognitum est, neque argenti scrupulum esse ullum in ea insula, neque ullam spem praedae, nisi ex mancipiis, ex quibus nullos puto te literis aut musicis eruditos expectare. Unus Birdus omnes Anglos ab hoc convicio prorsus liberat.*

lips, but prevent her with Thine everlasting blessing, and give her a long life, even for ever and ever, Amen.'[1] By substituting names, the same anthem was used for James and even for Charles I.

Although the Elizabethan age saw the perfection of the verse anthem, in which certain sections are entrusted to solo voices, the principle is, in fact, very little different from that used in nearly all of the Marian motets of pre-Reformation times. They too had their sections intended for soloists alternating with the richer sonorities of the full choir. Again continuity is apparent; and the comparison is by no means weakened by the use of instruments for the accompaniment of verse anthems, for instruments too were used (though they are usually unspecified) in the Henrician motets. An Italian from Treviso, writing home his impressions of a Chapel Royal service in 1514, says: 'after the procession High Mass commenced and was performed with great pomp, and with vocal and *instrumental* music, which lasted until 1 p.m.'[2]

This casual mention of the time of day serves to recall the tremendous differences in length between musical settings of the Ordinary of the Mass at the beginning and end of the century. A Fayrfax Mass consisting only of Gloria, Credo, Sanctus and Benedictus, and Agnus Dei takes nearly three-quarters of an hour to sing; yet each of Byrd's three Masses, which contain Kyries in addition, take roughly half that amount of time. The discrepancy is not due to any change or curtailment of Catholic ceremonial, but rather to a new musical outlook, in which æsthetic as well as liturgical considerations count for much.

On the whole, the latter part of Elizabeth's reign was a fairly safe haven for musicians. They could think and believe as they pleased, and they could write what pleased them. In setting the Communion service, they had to provide music for the Kyrie and Creed only; and for Morning and Evening Service the canticles were Venite, Te Deum, Benedictus (or Jubilate), and Magnificat and Nunc Dimittis. Outside this framework, there was ample opportunity for the composition of anthems, or (if inspiration were lacking) for the adaptation of Latin motets to English words. Thus Taverner's technique of adaptation was revived, but for a reason different by far from that professed by its inventor.

[1] *Tudor Church Music*, II, p. 266. [2] *Calendar of State Papers, Venetian*, II, p. 178.

II

The Ordinary of the Mass

The history of polyphonic settings of the Ordinary of the Mass in Tudor days is both complex and remarkable. Various politico-religious disturbances made the pattern of development much less clear and orderly than it might have been, since the Ordinary of the Mass is looked upon as a relatively unchanging liturgical entity, and one which might well have engendered a steady succession of English Masses conforming to one type and style, in so far as the primary characteristics of the form are concerned. Those Masses which have come down to us, either in their complete state or (as is often the case) lacking one, two, or even all but one voice-part, display an interesting lack of uniformity which almost calls for a minute subdivision of every single type. The diversity of liturgical observance must have contributed greatly towards the conditions which produced this very lack of uniformity, and it is hardly surprising to find such diversity criticized in the Book of Common Prayer, where the Use of Salisbury, Hereford, Bangor, York, and Lincoln are once and for all time swept away—'now from henceforth all the whole realm shall have but one Use'.

The Tudor Mass established itself upon the slenderest of traditions, and after rising to great musical heights it suddenly vanished (as was bound to happen) until it re-appeared under the stalwart though circumspect aegis of William Byrd. In a period of less than fifty years, from the beginning of the sixteenth century, or the last decade of the fifteenth, until the troubled times when abbeys and monasteries were being despoiled to provide royal treasure, the Mass proved itself a vehicle for splendid and reverent musical adornment. In the hands of such masters as Dunstable, Power and Benet,[1] a similar reputation had been built up in the early years of the fifteenth century; but between the death of Dunstable and the riper years of Fayrfax, Ludford, and Taverner, there was very little to show in the field of integrated, cyclic settings of

[1] For a special study of Benet, and a list of his works, see Brian Trowell, *Some English Contemporaries of Dunstable*, in *Proceedings of the Royal Musical Association*, 81 (1954–5), p. 77.

23

the Mass. This phenomenon, so common in insular sources, is reflected with great clarity in the seven choirbooks at Trent, which include less and less English music as the volumes progress. The earliest years of the Tudor dynasty apparently knew no other music for the Ordinary of the Mass than the three- and four-voiced compositions of Walter Frye and Richard Cox,[1] and the anonymous Mass in the Chapel Royal manuscript, now part of the Egerton collection in the British Museum.[2]

Frye's Masses, along with one by Cox, are preserved in a choirbook in the Royal Library of Brussels. Although all four works may have been written on the continent, they exhibit certain English characteristics which stamp them as being well apart from the main stream of Franco-Flemish sacred polyphony. Two Masses make use of the Kyrie trope *Deus creator omnium*, whose presence in Dufay's *Caput* Mass has given rise to the suggestion that even Dufay may have based his composition on an English model.[3] For *Deus creator omnium* is an important Sarum trope, the one designated for all Principal Doubles—the Feasts of the Nativity, the Epiphany, Easter Day, Ascension Day, Whitsun Day, the Assumption, the Anniversary of the Place, and the Dedication of a Church.

The widespread fame of this Kyrie trope is demonstrated by its occurrence in an organ Mass by a Welsh composer, Philip ap Rhys,[4] and in a four-part Mass by the Scot, Robert Carver, who uses the slightly varied version *Pater creator omnium*. Both

[1] Frye and Cox (Cockx) are discussed in Sylvia Kenney's article *Origins and Chronology of the Brussels Manuscript 5557 in the Bibliothèque royale de Belgique*, in *Revue Belge de Musicologie*, VI (1952), p. 75.

[2] The Mass is transcribed in the article by Manfred Bukofzer, *A Newly Discovered 15th-century Manuscript of the English Chapel Royal*, in *The Musical Quarterly*, XXXIII (1947), p. 38.

[3] See particularly Manfred Bukofzer, *Caput Redivivum: A New Source for Dufay's Missa Caput*, in *Journal of the American Musicological Society*, IV (1951), p. 97, and Frank Harrison, *An English 'Caput'*, in *Music and Letters*, XXXIII (1952), p. 203.

[4] Printed in *Altenglische Orgelmusik* (ed. D. W. Stevens), published by Bärenreiter (in England, Novello & Co. Ltd.).

use not only the verbal text (as Frye and Cox did) but also the proper chant for the trope, as a cantus firmus. Nevertheless, it is true to say that the polyphonic Kyrie never became fashionable in England, and consequently most insular Masses begin with '[Gloria in excelsis Deo] et in terra pax'. The reason for the omission of the Kyrie is bound up with liturgical practice and the demands of ceremonial customs, as well as the availability of a rich and varied repertoire of tropes. It so happened that the Kyrie occurred when there was a momentary lull in the ceremonies at High Mass: the priest, preceded by his ministers and acolytes, approached the altar to the singing of the Introit and Psalm, and after the Introit had been repeated, *Gloria Patri* was sung. Then followed the Confession, Absolution, the Kiss of Peace, the bringing of bread and wine and water for the Eucharist, and the blessing of incense. The Introit was repeated for the third and last time, and the Kyrie followed.

During the singing of Introit and Kyrie, the priest and his ministers were to sit in the sedilia and wait until the choir finished. Even plainsong for Introit and Kyrie would take up two or three minutes: a ninefold polyphonic Kyrie about ten minutes. This was clearly far too long a time to have to wait, and accordingly harmonized settings of Kyrie were discouraged.[1] It is noticeable, however, that as the sixteenth century progressed, composers began to write *alternatim* Kyries as a kind of compromise. A typical example, by Christopher Tye, provides polyphony for the second,

fourth, sixth, and eighth invocations, the remaining five being sung to the implied plainchant, which is *Orbis factor*.[2] Tye does not use the text of the trope—only the melody, and that in a highly elaborated form. The two Kyrie invocations are for four

[1] The fact that late fourteenth-century sources preserve Kyrie settings, both troped and untroped, indicates that a reaction took place during the early part of the fifteenth century. This reaction in favour of less complex musico-liturgical forms corresponds in some measure with the contemporary simplification of contrapuntal idiom and a noticeable slowing-up of harmonic rhythm.

[2] British Museum, Add. Ms. 17802-5.

voices, while the intervening sections set to 'Christe eleison' are given to a duo and a trio respectively. The complete Kyrie would require four or five minutes in perform, ance, and would thus appear to satisfy both æsthetic and practical demands. William Mundy, Hyett, Shepherd, and Taverner were among the other composers who compromised in the same way as Tye did.

Among the very few Masses containing a Kyrie are *Surrexit pastor bonus* (Lupus Italus),[1] the *Mass for a Meane* (Appleby), and the Masses by William Mundy and William Byrd. The remaining four sections, Gloria, Credo, Sanctus, and Agnus Dei, are found in practically every Tudor Mass, and this was regarded as a standard group, ing in much the same way as the four-movement symphony was to become an accep, ted form in more recent times. Single Mass-sections are found very occasionally, and they usually imply the loss of the other three members, rather than their suppression. Such is the case with a Kyrie and Gloria by Turges, a composer of the early years of the sixteenth century.[2]

It was the custom for most polyphonic settings of Gloria and Credo to begin at 'et in terra pax' and 'Patrem omnipotentem' respectively, the intonations being sung by the celebrant. There are, however, certain divergencies from this practice. Both of Mundy's Masses *Upon the Square* begin the Credo at 'factorem caeli'; so too does the four-part Mass *Pater creator omnium* by Robert Carver.[3] The works by Mundy also contain slightly different schemes for Sanctus and Agnus, which it was the custom to set complete. The first 'Sanctus' is intoned, and Mundy begins his poly, phonic setting at 'Sanctus, Sanctus Dominus Deus Sabaoth'. Similarly, the first 'Agnus Dei' is intoned, in accordance with strict liturgical custom.

The treatment of the text of *Credo in unum Deum* in the majority of Tudor Masses would appear to be somewhat less strict, for omission of certain phrases was frequent and by no means confined to one composer or one period.[4] The latter part of the Credo, from 'et resurrexit tertia die' to the end, is the usual place for omissions, although John Shepherd, in his Masses *Be not afraid*, *The Western Wynde* and *The French Mass*,[5] omits the phrase 'Deum de Deo . . . de Deo vero'. Indeed, his treat,

---

[1] In the Henrician set of part-books at Peterhouse, Cambridge. See Dom Anselm Hughes, *Catalogue of the Musical Manuscripts at Peterhouse, Cambridge*. The Masses by Appleby and Mundy are to be found in the set of part-books mentioned below (footnote 5). [2] British Museum, Add. Ms. 5665.

[3] Edinburgh, National Library of Scotland, Ms. 5/1/15. To be published in *Robert Carver: Opera Omnia* (*Corpus Mensurabilis Musicae* 16).

[4] The first survey of this problem was made by Dom Anselm Hughes, and appeared in the edition of *Missa O Quam Suavis*, prepared by H. B. Collins for the Plainsong and Medieval Music Society. For further discussions see Ruth Hannas, *Concerning Deletions in the Polyphonic Mass Credo*, in *Journal of the American Musicological Society*, V (1952), p. 155, and the reply by Jeremy Noble in the same journal, VI (1953), p. 91.

[5] All three are in B.M. Add. 17802-5. The *French Mass* has been edited by H. B. Collins (J. & W. Chester, Ltd.).

ment of the texts is extraordinarily unorthodox, for he even omits phrases from the Gloria. There are at least ten different Credo omissions, some long and some short, but it is significant to note that composers do not adhere to any single pattern of omission. Taverner and Ludford, for example, use three each, and Ludford is note- worthy (along with Mundy, Rasar, Lupus Italus, and Whitbroke) for setting the entire text without any omissions. It has been shown that the troped polyphonic Kyrie was discouraged owing to the amount of time taken to sing it, and a similar conclusion must be reached after considering the many conflicting reasons for omit- ting clauses in the Credo.

Political and religious arguments may at times have affected the structure of the liturgy, even to the extent of altering texts of great sanctity and significance, but as far as the Tudor Mass is concerned it is clear that the Credo omissions were made for the sake of time. The opulent and melismatic style of the Henrician period did much to prevent composers from compressing texts into a small musical space. In Taverner's Mass *Corona spinea*, two treble voices sing florid passages on one vowel ('o' of 'Domini', in the Benedictus) for approximately a minute, before changing to the next syllable.[1] This example is far from being exceptional: it is a common manifestation of a latter-day 'jubilus' technique which the English inherited from fifteenth-century continental composers. This technique, which was in direct opposition to the *parlando* style prevalent in the fourteenth century, was bound to elongate even a normal text of relatively short length. Since the Credo has the longest text of the sung portions of the Ordinary, it had to be curtailed in order to match the other sections. In this connection it is interesting to note that Fayrfax, Taverner, Ludford and their contemporaries often went to some trouble to make the four sections of the polyphonic Mass fairly equal in length.

A less frequently found, but none the less significant feature of style in the Tudor Mass is the *alternatim* scheme, whose importance in the music for the Choir Office has already been emphasized. That it has its place in the Ordinary of the Mass has already been seen in the description of the isolated Kyrie settings by Tye and others. Tye, inci- dentally, carried the principles of alteration between chant and polyphony into the realm of the Proper, for he has left harmonized versions of certain interior strophes of the Sequence *Post partum virgo*.[2] The remaining strophes may originally have existed as polyphonic music for a larger number of voice-parts than the two small sections preserved, for it was the custom to collect three- and four-part sections of larger works for performance as vocal chamber-music in the home. Whether this be the case,

---

[1] *Tudor Church Music*, I, p. 181.

[2] The two sections, *Tellus flumina* and *Unde nostris eya fave votis* are contained in the Oxford manuscript, Christ Church 45, where the music is written in such a manner that the individual voice-parts face out- wards when the volume is placed open on a table.

or whether plainsong was used, it must be conceded that the *alternatim* scheme has a strong claim, especially since there is corroborative evidence in the Sequence *Fulgens praeclara*, composed by Thomas Preston for organ and plainchant.[1]

Continental practice corresponds in main outlines to English practice where alternation is concerned, and there is a further link in the fact that its use is comparatively infrequent. A Gloria by Dufay, five Masses by Isaac, and the Mantuan Masses by Palestrina are the most celebrated works in this genre.[2] In England, there are the seven Masses by Ludford, Shepherd's *Mass for a Meane*, and two of the York Masses, which form convincing Gloria-Credo pairs. The Masses by Ludford[3] are all for three voices, and are preserved in three part-books. A fourth book contains those parts of the Ordinary destined to be sung—or even played by an elaborating organist—alternately with the polyphony. Ludford shows much contrapuntal felicity in managing three-voiced texture; yet in doing so he seems to be looking back rather than forward, echoing as it were the sparse and solemn sounds of the fifteenth century, of *Rex seculorum*, *Grüne Linden*, and *O rosa bella*.

Shepherd, in contrast to Ludford (who sets all the movements in *alternatim* style) has only the Gloria and Credo broken up in this way.[4] Once again there is divergence as to what phrases are given to polyphonists, and what to the singers of plainchant, just in the same way as there was divergence in the length and location of Credo omissions. Turning now to the York Masses,[5] it is interesting to compare the one alternating Kyrie with those previously discussed, for the scheme is exactly the same: invocations 2, 4, 6, and 8 are set for choir, and the remaining ones are to be chanted. The composer is William Horwood, two of whose compositions survive complete in the Eton choirbook.

The first of the two short alternatim Masses (both are anonymous) has a slightly retrospective air, with complex and inconsistent notation giving more than a hint of some late Plantagenet amateur. The second Mass is, by contrast, very straightforward from a notational point of view, and makes considerable use of imitative patterns and smoothly-flowing counterpoint. This Mass is based upon a short versicle *Custodi nos, Domine*, sung immediately after the hymn at Compline, and here provided with a

[1] For a discussion of this sequence, see Denis Stevens, *Further Light on Fulgens Praeclara*, in *Journal of the American Musicological Society*, IX (1956), p. 1.

[2] The Dufay Gloria is printed in *Denkmäler der Tonkunst in Österreich*, XXXI, p. 81. For the Isaac Masses see the edition by Louise Cuyler (University of Michigan Press). Palestrina's *alternatim* Masses are discussed by Jeppesen, *The Recently Discovered Mantova Masses of Palestrina*, in *Acta Musicologica*, XXII (1950), p. 36.

[3] British Museum Roy. App. 45–48. For further information on Nicholas Ludford see the articles by Hugh Baillie in *The Musical Quarterly*, XLIV (1958), p. 196, and by John D. Bergsagel in *Musica Disciplina*, XIV (1960).

[4] British Museum, Add. Mss. 17802–5.

[5] See Hugh Baillie and Philippe Oboussier, *The York Masses*, in *Music and Letters*, XXXV (1954), p. 19. In all probability this music was originally intended for use in London.

decorative cauda. In the Gloria the predominant texture is four-part, and cadences use the total number of voices for every verse. But the layout of the Credo is more elaborate: after two four-part verses there comes a duo for treble and bass ('Et incarnatus') followed by a trio for 'Et ascendit':

A noteworthy insular feature of Tudor Masses is the range of texture and the choice of voice-parts. There are no Masses extant for less than three voices or more than ten, and the credit for spanning this wide range goes to the Scottish composer, Robert Carver, sometime canon of Scone Abbey in Perthshire. He wrote Masses for three, four, five, six and ten voices. The usual choice of Tudor composers was for five voices ranging from treble to bass, but occasionally special circumstances called for unusual resources, and the result was that a small number of works are set 'for a meane', that is for a counter-tenor, whose part is usually the highest of four. Two Masses by Thomas Appleby and John Shepherd have this title in the manuscript sources which have come down to us; other works, however, have equal claim to the title, since their highest part is comfortably within alto range. Tallis's four-part Mass[1] is an obvious and readily available example, and another (this time five-part) Mass equally suitable for men's voices is *Sine nomine* by John Taverner.[2] Masses of this type were undoubtedly very useful when choirboys were away, the men being left to sing the polyphonic parts of the service on their own.

In considering the wide variety of types which exists in the Tudor Mass, it is important to realize that a very great number of Masses rely on a cantus firmus, whose normal position is in the tenor part. The cantus firmus, when liturgical, gave the work its *raison d'être*, since the feast for which the Mass was intended was usually represented by an antiphon or respond from the Office of the day. The plainchant thus chosen would be elongated, and possibly broken up, in order to form a definite mensural scheme. If the plainsong were long, as in the antiphon *O quam suavis* used for the Mass of that name, it would not appear very often in its complete form. In fact

---

[1] *Tudor Church Music*, VI, p. 31.
[2] *idem*, I, p. 50. The correct title is *Meane Mass* (i.e. for a choir whose highest voices are counter-tenors).

it appears only twice in this particular Mass, which recent research has shown to be very probably the work of John Lloyd.[1] A shorter plainsong, such as *Corona spinea*, appears ten times during the course of Taverner's Mass for the Feast of the Crown of our Lord. The composer was thus free in the first instance to choose a plainsong which would serve as a scaffold for his polyphony, but having once chosen it, he would be bound by its length to a greater or lesser number of repetitions.

The normal practice was to allow the cantus firmus to appear only during the sections for full choir. Other sections in duo or trio would make use of independent motives. There were, of course, many exceptions to this general rule, since Tudor composers followed the dictates of their own musical conscience rather than a set formula or method of composition. As an additional piece of unifying structural aid, composers nearly always made use of a short phrase common to the beginnings of all four sections of the Mass. It has become the custom in recent years to call this a head-motive, a term derived from the German *Kopfmotiv*. This term is quite suitable provided it is clearly understood that the motive is not merely a melodic tag: it is a polyphonic segment, and recurs as such at the beginning of Gloria, Credo, Sanctus and Agnus Dei. Most Tudor composers appear to have used it instinctively, though by no means indiscriminately. Fayrfax, for example, uses a head-motive for his Mass *Tecum principium*, but the separate voice-parts of the motive are gradually decorated as the Mass proceeds, so that when Agnus Dei is reached the motive as such is hardly recognizable.

Among the many Masses conforming to this type, which combined cantus firmus and head-motive, are those of Alwood, Ashwell, Jones, Knight, Ludford, Lloyd, Lupus, Aston, Fayrfax, Taverner, and Carver. The cantus firmus of Alwood's Mass[2] consists of only five notes (see Ex. 8) repeated in varying rhythmical combinations, the final 'dona nobis pacem' being moulded upon a quintuple scheme. The title of this Mass, *Praise Him Praiseworthy*, may have been derived from a para-liturgical source, for the five syllables fit the five notes of the theme and may originally have been associated with it. Ashwell's Mass *Ave Maria*[3] draws upon the plainchant antiphon of the same name, and contains a very rare example of double gymel in the Gloria, where trebles and altos are both divided at one point, giving a complete and rich harmonic effect of high tessitura. This treatment of the phrase 'qui tollis peccata mundi' is also to be found at the same place in another Mass by the same composer, based this time upon a short respond for Prime in Easter week, *Jesu Christe*.[4] Dunstable's Mass *Jesu Christe*[5] is, incidentally, indebted to a cognate plainsong,

---

[1] Thurston Dart, *Cambrian Eupompus*, in *The Listener*, no. 1359, March 17, 1955, p. 497.
[2] In the Forrest-Heyther part-books, Oxford, Bodleian Library, Ms. Mus. Sch. E 376–381, no. 18.
[3] *idem*, no. 13. [4] *idem*, no. 10.
[5] *John Dunstable: Complete Works*, ed. M. F. Bukofzer (*Musica Britannica*, VIII), p. 35.

though the source is slightly different, and is used only in Ascensiontide. The Masses by Jones (*Spes noster*), Knight (*Libera nos*) and Lupus (*Surrexit pastor bonus*) are unfortunately defective, owing to a missing part-book,[1] but they certainly owe their titles to plainchant cantus firmi. Ludford, in his Mass for the Feast of the Annunciation (*Christi Virgo*) indulges in brilliant and florid part-writing which must have taxed the powers of his singers very severely. A more sober, though none the less brilliant testimony of his powers as a contrapuntist is the Mass *Videte miraculum*[2] which makes use of the respond so named for the Feast of the Purification.

Ex.8   ALWOOD

Other Masses by Ludford belong to this type, as well as all the known Masses of Robert Fayrfax, who was his greatest contemporary.[3] Fayrfax has long been noted for his fluid, luminous counterpoint, which seems to combine the virtues of the late fifteenth-century school with the newly-found powers of a younger generation. He must have had access to earlier sources, and certainly knew Dunstable's motet *Albanus roseo*, for the beautiful but recondite theme used in this motet appears in his Mass *Albanus*, and is there subjected to a remarkable treatment involving total inversion and retrograde movement. The theme is taken from an antiphon which appears in a rhymed office for St. Alban. Two other Masses, *Regali* and *Tecum principium*, are built upon antiphons, for the Conception of the B.V.M. and for the Feast of the

[1] The Henrician set at Peterhouse, Cambridge. The Lupus Mass derives from a motet by Andrea de Silva, as Lewis Lockwood has shown (*Music & Letters*, XLII (1961) pp. 341 ff.).

[2] This Mass, together with *Christi Virgo*, is in the Caius choirbook.

[3] See Dom Anselm Hughes, *An Introduction to Fayrfax*, in *Musica Disciplina*, VI (1952), p. 83, and two articles by Edwin B. Warren, *The Life and Works of Robert Fayrfax*, in *Musica Disciplina*, XI (1957) p. 134; *The Masses of Robert Fayrfax*, idem, XII (1958), p. 145.

Nativity. The treatment of the head-motive in the latter work has already been discussed; in the former, it is normal and regular.

Taverner came as a worthy successor to Fayrfax, and inherited many of the earlier master's technical traits.[1] There is little in the way of padding in his gracious and limpid melismata: each phrase is imbued with a life of its own, each sequence has an artistic climax and a graceful cadence. The most important of his cantus firmus Masses are *Corona spinea*, *O Michael*, and *Gloria tibi Trinitas*. The first of these has already been mentioned in connection with Taverner's vocal style; it is a work on the largest possible scale, and suggests that the Feast of the Crown of our Lord, although added at a fairly late stage in the Sarum Kalendar, was held in special esteem at Tattershall or Oxford, where Taverner spent most of his working life. The Mass *O Michael* is not, as its name suggests, for the principal feast of St. Michael on September 29th; the cantus firmus (most unusually) has a different incipit from the title of the Mass. It is the respond *Archangeli Michaelis*, sung at procession on the Feast of St. Michael in Monte Tumba, which took place on October 16th. The 'O' in the title of the Mass may therefore stand for October: it is certainly not an invocation. *Gloria tibi Trinitas* takes its name from an antiphon sung at Second Vespers on Trinity Sunday, and it has achieved recent fame through being revealed as the unwitting progenitor of a century and a half of English chamber music:[2] the 'In nomine' compositions which lasted until the time of Purcell were nearly all based upon the same antiphon, as it appeared in the 'in nomine Domini' section of Taverner's Benedictus.

It would be tempting to continue this survey of the mainstream of Mass settings in Tudor times, but there are certain tributaries which demand attention, and they are still, almost inevitably, connected with the cantus firmus principle. An important group in its own right is the small number of works based on a secular or para-liturgical cantus firmus. English composers showed considerably less enthusiasm than their continental contemporaries when it was a question of bringing in a secular tune. There is, for instance, only one example of a Mass on *L'homme armé*—that by Robert Carver[3]—although dozens exist in Europe. Shepherd, Taverner, and Tye all wrote four-part Masses on *The Western Wynde*, and it has been said that Carver too based his three-part Mass on this secular song.[4] The first few notes of the theme do, in fact, occur in the treble part of Carver's Mass, but the resemblance goes no further than

[1] His Masses are printed in *Tudor Church Music*, I. The *Mass Western Wynde* is published separately in an edition by Philip Brett (Stainer & Bell).

[2] Gustave Reese, *The Origin of the English In Nomine*, in *Journal of the American Musicological Society*, II (1949), p. 7.

[3] *Music of Scotland* (ed. K. Elliott, *Musica Britannica*, XV), p. 30.

[4] Farmer, *A History of Music in Scotland*, p. 109.

this, and seems to be purely coincidental. Tye's Mass, on the other hand, gives the complete theme to the altos throughout the work, and they sing it no less than twenty-nine times. This feat of endurance may have been intended as a musical ripost

to Taverner, who gives the tune to all the voices in turn except the altos. A secular origin may also be assumed for the themes of Ashwell's *God save King Harry* and Taverner's *Small Devotion* (not *In All Devotion*, as some pretend).[1] The name *Be Not Afraid*, which Shepherd may possibly have taken from the Bible, has no more liturgical significance than the title of his *French Mass*, which simply refers to the style in which the music was composed.

The so-called Playnsong Masses by Shepherd and Taverner are, by an odd twist of irony, not based on plainsong at all; they rely upon straightforward chordal counterpoint, with very little elaboration. Burton's Mass *Ut re mi fa sol la* speaks for itself; the hexachord theme, beginning on *f*, rises to *d* and then falls again to the *f*. The Masses *Upon the Square* by Munday and Whitbroke have been variously and ingeniously explained; the true explanation, however, is bound up with square notation. Certain models in cantus fractus were used by these two composers (and by the anonymous composer of two Kyries in John Baldwin's manuscript) and more or less decorated according to the needs of the music. These 'square' sources go back to the early fifteenth century, and provide another link between the schools of Dunstable and Fayrfax.

Few examples of *contrafacta* or parody Masses have so far been discovered in England: this technique, like that of using a secular cantus firmus, had apparently not gained a firm footing in Tudor England. The first authenticated example of a parody Mass is usually thought to be *O bone Jesu*, which Fayrfax based upon a motet

[1] In view of the fact that *Small Devotion* is a musical derivation of the motet *Christe Jesu*, originally in honour of St. William of York (and later adapted for Wolsey, Henry VIII, and Elizabeth), the title may well be a corruption of 'S. will. devocio'. See article on Taverner in *Die Musik in Geschichte und Gegenwart*.

(similarly named) of his own composition. Only one voice-part of the motet survives, but it is enough to show the link between the two works. Later parodies survive in Taverner's Mass *Small Devotion* (based on his motet *Christe Jesu pastor bone*) and the Mass and motet on *Salve intemerata Virgo*, by Tallis.

The very small category of Masses without cantus firmus contains three of the most famous settings of all: the Masses for three, four, and five voices by Byrd.[1] These Masses were probably written towards the end of Elizabeth's reign, and were published early in the reign of James I. A copy of the three-part Mass in Baldwin's manuscript follows a piece dated 1603; this may refer merely to the date of copying, and not of composition. All three Masses make use of a head-motive, although this use is irregular. One motive appears in all incipits of the three-part Mass, except the Sanctus. Two motives are used for the Mass *a 4*, Credo alone being unaffected, while the Mass *a 5* has a similar arrangement of paired motives, in which the Sanctus is once again formed of separate melodic material. Each Mass has a Kyrie. Tallis's four-part Mass also uses head-motives, and is almost unique in being a parody upon itself, since all the sections of the Gloria from 'propter magnam gloriam tuam' onwards appear in the succeeding sections, with only very small and insignificant changes.[2] Carver's Masses *a 3* and *a 6* lack cantus firmus but are unified by head-motives, and the same is true of Taverner's *Sine nomine (Meane Mass)*.

[1] Printed in *Tudor Church Music*, IX, also available in various separate editions.
[2] The 'lost' Mass *a 7* by Tallis, of which sections from Tenbury Mss. 341-4 were printed in *Tudor Church Music*, VI, pp. 49-61, can now be largely completed thanks to several concordances established by Dr. Joseph Kerman. The cantus firmus of this Mass has been identified by Mr. Jeremy Noble as the Christmas Introit, *Puer natus est nobis*.

III

The Motet

The term 'motet' is generally used nowadays in contradistinction to the term 'anthem', yet at one time their roles were almost exactly reversed, and the latter term (variously spelt as 'antemne', 'antempe' and so forth) referred quite clearly to a polyphonic composition that would now be classified as a motet. It is somewhat unfortunate that this all-embracing word has been used, especially during the past century, in a loose and misleading manner, so that by a process which is literally a reduction to the absurd, every piece of vocal polyphony not part of the Ordinary of the Mass has been dubbed 'motet'. Although a similar confusion exists in sixteenth-century publications and inventories, this is hardly an excuse for the perpetuation in modern editions of such a haphazard state of affairs. Even the august and scholarly volumes of *Tudor Church Music* give very sparse indications of the real liturgical background to the wide variety of works included. Antiphons, responds, hymns, sequences, and many other important liturgical forms are carelessly classed with large-scale extra-liturgical compositions (usually in honour of the Virgin) as 'motets', which some of them are not, and never could have been. The true and only criterion is, of course, the verbal text; if this is to be found in antiphoners, graduals, and processionals, a liturgical occasion can be assigned with reasonable accuracy to the work in question. If the text does not appear in these sources, then the music almost certainly belongs to some occasion no less devout, but nevertheless outside the actual liturgy.

The hymns and psalms of the daily office, or canonical hours of prayer, were usually sung to the appointed plainsong. Polyphonic music entered the ceremonies rarely, except during Matins, Vespers, and Compline. At Matins, it was the hymn *Te Deum* which was most frequently set in polyphony; at Vespers, *Magnificat* held pride of place. But it was after Compline, and sometimes even after Vespers, that the most elaborate musical offering of the day was made—an antiphon, set in the most resplendent and sonorous polyphony, was sung in honour of the Virgin. The Sarum form of Compline contained none of the four Marian antiphons which have always been an important part of this service in the Roman rite. The singing of these antiphons was, however, frequently prescribed by special statutes of colleges, guilds, and cathedrals, either as part of the Hours of the Blessed Virgin, or as an evening devotion to her. The statutes for Henry VI's foundations of King's College, Cambridge, and Eton College prescribe the singing of an antiphon every evening; in the case of Eton the title of the antiphon for Lent—*Salve regina*—appears in the statute itself.[1] Outside Lent, any other antiphon in honour of the Virgin was allowed to be sung. *Salve regina* was also prescribed in Thomas Elys's foundation deed for the chantry of St. Thomas the Martyr at Sandwich,[2] and as a matter of course in the statutes of the chantry established in the church of St. Magnus, London Bridge, where there existed a guild 'de Salve Regina' from the reign of Edward III.[3]

In the earliest and perhaps the greatest collection of Tudor motets, the Eton choir-book, there were fifteen settings of *Salve regina*, ranging from five to nine voice-parts. The next most frequently set text was *Gaude flore virginali*, a hymn in commemoration of the Five Joys of the Virgin. The first word of this hymn came to denote the candles, or 'gawdyes', which were lit before the image of the Virgin during the singing of the antiphon. Other hymns to the Virgin in the Eton choir book are *Gaude Virgo mater Christi* (three settings, with a fourth which diverges after the incipit into a different poem), *Guade Virgo salutata*, *O regina celestis glorie* and *Stella celi*, a hymn against the plague, beseeching the Virgin for divine protection.[4]

The style of these Marian motets—for they are motets in the proper sense of the word—is noble and pious, yet full of contrast and complexity. *Salve regina* is troped[5] (that is, provided with extra verses, usually sung by soloists) in many of the early Tudor settings: Browne, Cornyshe, Davy, Fayrfax, Hacomplaynt, Hampton, Howchyn, Hygons, Lambe, Ludford, Sutton, and Wylkynson are among the many

[1] Harrison, *The Eton Choirbook*, in *Annales Musicologiques*, I (1953), p. 158.
[2] W. Boys, *Collections for an History of Sandwich*, p. 192.
[3] J. Stow, *A Survey of London*, II, p. 175.
[4] The ever-recurring danger of the plague in the later Middle Ages may have been one of the causes for the fairly frequent musical settings, in England, of *Stella celi*, which was sung to its own chant both in England and on the continent. The earliest known polyphonic setting is that by Cooke, in the Old Hall Manuscript. Roughly contemporary with Lambe's setting (in the Eton Choirbook) are those by Sir William Hawte (B.M. Add. Ms. 5665—which also contains a second, anonymous, setting) and Dr. Cooper (B.M. Royal App. 58). There is a later composition by Thorne in the Baldwin Ms. (RM 24 d 2).
[5] These tropes were rediscovered just over a century ago by Dr. Rock, who mentioned them in the original edition of his book, *The Church of Our Fathers* (see revised edition, p. 209, footnote 71). There were five verses in all, but the usual practice was to set only the first three. Two exceptions occur in the Eton Choirbook: Wylkynson's five-part setting has verse 5 instead of verse 3, and Hampton's has verse 5 following verse 3. In the Scone Choirbook the fourth verse (*Gloriosa Dei Mater*) makes a unique appearance in the second of the two *Salve regina* settings.

composers who used the troped version of this antiphon, the performance of which must have lasted nearly a quarter of an hour. Some of the settings are based on cantus firmi taken from the office of Feasts of the Blessed Virgin, or from other important liturgical occasions: compositions by Browne and Hygons can both be connected with Maundy Thursday,[1] while Sutton's seven-part setting is based on an antiphon for Trinity Sunday.[2]

After a text had achieved wide currency, it became the fashion to change certain features while yet relating the sense and sentiment to the adoration of the Virgin. Ludford, for example, has set the text *Salve regina pudica mater*, and Fawkyner the text *Salve regina vas mundicie*.[3] Similar changes were wrought upon *Ave Maria*, which in the hands of Arthur Chamberlayne became 'Ave gratia plena Maria tecum Dominus' . . . and in John Mason's setting 'Ave fuit prima salus . . . Maria dum salutaris . . . Gratia sancti spiritus . . . Plena tu es virtutibus'.[4] Each word of the anti-phon became the initial word of a short sentence, and each of these sentences is separated by an acclamation *Ave Maria*, so that the final effect is that of a trope within a trope. Tallis, in his *Ave rosa sine spinis*[5] (see Ex. 10), has troped the antiphon in such a way as to transform it into a Marian motet of almost symphonic proportions. Indeed, nearly all of the motets in honour of the Virgin are extended in length besides being extensive, and they are set out for five or more voice-parts in the richest possible polyphony. A very great number of different texts was used, some being metrical hymns, others sequences or proses. The presence of a cantus firmus was felt to be less

Ex.10   TALLIS

[1] *The Eton Choirbook*, I, p. 124; II, p. 39.

[2] *Idem*, II, p. 1.

[3] This six-part motet is one of the many compositions now unfortunately missing from the Eton Choir-book.

[4] These two works are to be found in the Henrician part-books at Peterhouse, Cambridge.

[5] *Tudor Church Music*, VI, p. 169. This motet, with the missing portions completed by the present writer, has been broadcast on the BBC Third Programme, by the Schola Polyphonica (Director, Henry Washington).

and less obligatory as the century wore on, so that compositions similar in all other respects to the earlier types no longer anchored themselves to plainchant: Johnson's *Gaude Maria Virgo*, Carver's *Gaude flore virginali*, and Tallis's *Salve intermerata Virgo* are all examples of this newer style of composition. Yet at the other end of the scale stands Lambe's *O regina celestis glorie*, which is built upon two distinct cantus firmi sung simultaneously. Its structural layout and high degree of technical competence recall a work written only a decade or so later—the motet *Optime pastor* which Isaac wrote for the accession of Pope Leo X.[1]

Worship of the Virgin inspired not only a large number of settings of *Magnificat*, but even affected *Te Deum*, which was sometimes given the paraphrastic text *Te matrem Dei laudamus*, Aston's work being the best known and most readily accessible.[2] *Magnificat*, on the other hand, was considered to be one of the most sacred of all texts, and was never troped or altered in any way. It was almost invariably composed for alternating plainsong and polyphony, and since the plainsong for the canticle was so well-known, the custom was to give only the polyphonic verses, which began 'et exultavit'. The great choirbooks of Eton, Caius, Lambeth and Edinburgh are rich in settings of *Magnificat*,[3] and significantly enough the part-books of the mid-sixteenth century are correspondingly poor due to the gradual suppression of Mariolatry by Cranmer and the reformers. In its finest and most imposing settings, the canticle of the Virgin was almost a personal offering or prayer of the composer himself; and no composer of the Henrician period, whether famous or humble, neglected to write a *Magnificat*. It was a solemn duty, and the result was often a solemn and impressive polyphonic canvas, set off by a framework of plainsong verses which

---

[1] The two simultaneously used cantus firmi are *Da pacem* and *Sacerdos et pontifex*.

[2] *Tudor Church Music*, X, p. 99. The Marian form of the text is reproduced on p. xxi.

[3] The Eton Choirbook alone contained 24 settings, ranging from four to seven voice-parts; of these 24, 15 are now completely missing.

served both to heighten contrast and to give relief to the ear. The examples by Fayrfax, Ludford, Cornyshe, Appleby, and Jones all display a sure yet flexible technique, and in spite of their strength and solidarity they contain gracious melodic lines and sensitive counterpoint. They rarely have the plainchant (to which the odd-numbered verses are sung) as a cantus firmus throughout the entire work, though occasionally it appears at the beginning and end. Appleby, Darke and Taverner[1] use

this method, while Ludford and others prefer to hint at the plainchant by means of

[1] *Tudor Church Music,* III, p. 17.

strong melodic progressions in the tenor part. Byrd has left us no Latin setting of *Magnificat*, although there are two from the pen of his teacher, Thomas Tallis,[1] and fine examples by the elder Mundy, and by John Shepherd.

The principle of alternation was applied generously to hymn-tunes, and to a lesser extent to psalms. Hymns for Matins, Vespers and Compline, normally sung to plain-chant, were divided between the choir and the assembled priests or monks in such a way that the first verse and remaining odd-numbered verses were chanted, and the even verses sung in polyphony. A rubric from the Erlyngham Breviary[2] shows that this principle of alternation was built upon a hallowed liturgical practice of great antiquity: 'The ruler of the choir should begin the hymn as far as the second or third word; and the choir on the side of the officiating priest continue that verse, and the other part of the choir on the other side, the next verse; and so they alternate each verse to the end; which is to be observed throughout the whole year; the choir at the end of the last verse responding *Amen*.' The ruler of the choir was a priest who acted as liaison between precentor and choir. It was his duty to enquire the antiphon on the psalms, and the intonation of the psalm, from the precentor, and similarly to supervise the participation in hymns, canticles, and responsories.

In the same way that *Magnificat* was referred to by the opening words of its second verse 'et exultavit', so the hymns were listed by their second verse—a fact which has caused them to be re-edited and even published and recorded[3] in a misleading form. Thus *Hic nempe mundi gaudia*[4] is not a motet by Tallis, but a set of polyphonic verses for five-part choir, based on the plainchant hymn *Deus tuorum militum*. In the sixteenth century, the hymn was sung as follows:

Ruler	:	Deus tuorum militum	
Cantors	:	Sors et corona, praemium:	plainchant
		Laudes canentes Martyris,	
		Absolve nexu criminis.	
Choir	:	Hic nempe mundi gaudia . . .	polyphony
Cantors	:	Poenas cucurrit fortiter . . .	plainchant
Choir	:	Ob hoc precatu supplici . . .	polyphony
Cantors	:	Deo Patri sit gloria . . .	plainchant

Amen would probably have been sung by all present, but when the last verse happened to be set polyphonically, the *Amen* was often harmonized too. Shepherd and Tallis

---

[1] *Tudor Church Music*, VI, pp. 64, 73.

[2] Salisbury, Chapter Library, Ms. 152. The translation is from *The Psalter, or Seven Ordinary Hours of Prayer* (ed. J. D. Chambers, 1852), p. 62.

[3] In *The History of Music in Sound*, HMS 37 (also HLP 9 (III, 1)).

[4] *Tudor Church Music*, VI, p. 264. Attributed to Shepherd in Christ Church Mss. 979–83.

have both left settings of *Deus tuorum militum*, also of *Salvator mundi Domine, Jam Christus astra ascenderat*, and *Jesu salvator seculi*. There are several more alternatim hymns from the pen of John Shepherd, and three different ones besides these from Thomas Tallis, who shows a tendency towards both economy and form by setting verse 4 of *Sermone blando angelus*[1] to the same music as verse 2, and similarly verse 8 to the music or verse 6. A decline in the popularity of cantus firmus verses and alternatim performance came about in the time of William Mundy and Byrd, probably after 1570, although a fine setting by Mundy of *A solis ortus cardine* is extant. Byrd composed alternatim versions of *Sacris sollemniis* and *Pange lingua*,[2] although his most famous hymn is a through-composed setting of *Christe qui lux*, in which the tune (sung in plainchant for the first and last verses) is given to each of the five voices in turn for the remainder of the hymn.

His alternatim hymns demonstrate with admirable clarity two entirely different methods of setting the chant: in *Sacris sollemniis* the three polyphonic verses keep the melody in the highest part, and always in even note-values. The other four parts are based on imitative figures melodically independent of the chant itself, except in the last verse, where they are indebted to the opening phrase (see Ex. 12). The plainchant of *Pange lingua*, on the other hand, is placed not at the top where it can be heard, but right in the middle of the texture, and even there it is further obscured by an extremely free treatment of the melodic line. White, in his *Christe qui lux*,[3] has

[1] *idem*, VI, p. 193.
[2] *idem*, IX, p. 248; VII, p. 134.
[3] *idem*, V, p. 176. See also the three preceding settings, p. 168ff.

a regular cantus firmus in the tenor, a voice which is rarely favoured in Tallis's hymns. Tallis prefers to entrust the melody to the highest voice, and his usual method is to decorate the melody slightly, often in compound duple rhythm, for the opening verses; and then to present it in even note-values and sober guise for the last verse.

Polyphonic psalm settings appear much more rarely than hymns during the early Tudor period, although notable exceptions show that similar technical processes were applied to complete psalms for important feasts. Experiments began in the reign of Henry VII with the erasure of alternate plainsong verses in liturgical books such as processionals and antiphoners, and the substitution of mensural notation for the chant. In one instance it has been possible to reconstruct an alternatim faburden scheme for the psalms *Laudate Dominum* and *In exitu Israel*, sung during the procession to the font at Vespers on Easter Day.[1] The same psalms have been set jointly by Shepherd, Thomas Byrd, and W. Mundy, and as all three were members of the Chapel Royal together it is quite possible that they may have collaborated in this way.

Texts from the Bible, and especially from the Psalms, replaced the Marian hymns and sequences which had been so popular with composers of the Fayrfax period. The non-liturgical and therefore motet style of these compositions is demonstrated by the fact that the entire psalm-text was set, but not the doxology. It is thus unlikely that they were used at Vespers or elsewhere in the Office, though they may well have served to bring about a musical, as opposed to a liturgical climax in the daily services of Elizabeth's Chapel Royal. Motets of this type never use a cantus firmus; their texture is a closely integrated mesh of imitative melodic fragments, worked out

[1] See the account of B. M. Harley Ms. 2945: Stevens, *Processional Psalms in Faburden*, in *Musica Disciplina*, IX (1955), p. 105.

with considerable skill and a high regard for individual voice-progressions. The examples by Tallis, W. Mundy, Byrd, Parsons, Shepherd and White, are typical and illustrative of the new motet style of the Elizabethan period.[1] Not only are the words of the text allowed to influence the music in a direct manner, whenever this is desirable and effective—they are even permitted a more humanistic function in reflecting the composer's own feelings.

Although examples of this extremely subjective treatment are rare, they are quite unmistakable when seen in the context of a normal psalm verse. W. Mundy's *Memor esto verbi tui* breaks forth into double gymel at the words 'Cantabiles mihi erant justificationes tuae'; and his son John Mundy, in a setting of *In te Domine speravi*, uses exactly the same technique—incidentally enlarging the texture to seven real parts—at the words 'Vide humilitatem meam et laborem meum'.[2] For sheer musical labour it would be difficult to better Tallis's *Spem in alium*, written in forty parts (for eight five-part choirs) and a musical monument of impressive sound and proportions.[3] Nevertheless, Tallis was not alone in having produced so vast a canvas, for Italian and Spanish composers of the sixteenth century exerted their contrapuntal ingenuity to similar ends.

Tallis and Byrd together composed and published the first collection of Latin motets ever to be printed in England—*Cantiones quae ab argumento Sacrae vocantur* (1575). The acceptance by Queen Elizabeth of the dedication of this work is not surprising in view of her support of the Latin Prayer Book, and her approval of services in Latin on special occasions and in special places.[4] The texts set by Byrd and Tallis are in any case non-controversial in that they contain nothing written in honour of the Virgin; but they are far from being non-liturgical, in spite of the number of settings in motet-style of psalm verses and Biblical texts. There are several hymns, a few settings of short antiphons (*Miserere mihi, Domine* by Byrd, and two versions of *Salvator mundi salva nos*, for Holy Cross Day, by Tallis) and several polyphonic elaborations of responsorial chant. Byrd's *Libera me*, with its two related sections, must alternate with plainchant, as must the short respond *Candidi facti sunt Nazarei*, composed by Tallis. A polyphonic responsory of greater stature is the same composer's *Honor virtus et potestas*, for Trinity Sunday.

This work is printed in *Tudor Church Music* (VI, p. 237) exactly as it appears in

---

[1] Twelve of these psalm-motets by Robert White are printed in *Tudor Church Music*, V. For similar works by Tallis, see *idem*, VI, pp. 116, 246.

[2] These two compositions are in Oxford, Christ Church, Ms. 979-83.

[3] *Tudor Church Music*, VI, p. 299.

[4] It has not hitherto been noticed that the dedication to Queen Elizabeth was stressed by both composers in a very subtle way. The year 1575, when the *Cantiones* were published, was the seventeenth year of Elizabeth's reign: hence the fact that Byrd and Tallis each contributed 17 items to the collection. Byrd's contributions are printed in *Tudor Church Music*, IX; Tallis's are *idem*, VI.

the part-books. All voice-parts begin with the word 'Virtus' which is really the second word of the responsory: the first word is 'Honor', and this should be intoned before the choir begins, using the correct plainsong at the same pitch as the tenor line of Tallis's composition. When the choir has reached the end of the polyphonic section, a small group of soloists sing the Verse *Trinitate laus perennis, Unitati sit decus perpetim.* Then the choir repeats the last section of the polyphony from 'In perenni' to the end. It will be noticed that there is a perfectly clear cadence immediately before the words 'In perenni', so that the repetenda makes a fresh and convincing musical start. Next the soloists sing *Gloria Patri et Filio, et Spiritui Sancto* to plainsong based on that of the Verse (and note that *Sicut erat* is never sung), and to round off the choir once more repeats from 'In perenni' to the end. In effect, the responsory resembles somewhat the rondo-form of later ages.

A similar scheme is apparent in Taverner's *Dum transisset Sabbatum* (III, p. 37) where the words 'Dum transisset' are wrongly underlaid. These two words should be

Ex.13   TAVERNER

intoned, and the polyphony should begin with the word 'Sabbatum', as may be proved by comparing the opening notes of the tenor part with the plainsong for the entire respond. The perfect cadence on 'aromata' will be noticed, for this as usual shows the beginning of the repetenda, 'Ut venientes'. An alternative and exactly opposite scheme is to have the soloists' portions exchanged with those of the choir, and this may be seen in Taverner's *In pace* (III, p. 48). The choir sings the incipit, soloists continue with *in idipsum: Dormiam et requiescam.* Next the choir sings from 'Si dedero' to 'dormitationem', and soloists repeat *Dormiam et requiescam. Gloria Patri* follows (in polyphony) by the choir, then they go back to *In pace.* Once more the soloists repeat *in idipsum: Dormiam et requiescam,* and the responsory is over.

In 1589 and 1591, Byrd, this time alone, published his two books of *Cantiones*

Sacrae.[1] Like the earlier collection, these were retrospective publications, containing works which had for years been circulated in manuscript copies, often defective and unreliable. The two books of *Gradualia*[2] (1605 and 1607) may well have been composed in the last years of Elizabeth's reign, and it is therefore possible to consider them as a part, if not the very summit, of the musical heritage of Tudor England. Although Byrd lived on until 1623, his training, technique, and outlook were nothing if not Elizabethan, and his music shows more clearly than most how slowly and yet how relentlessly he moved towards his ideal conception of the link between tonal art and liturgical function. He knew that perfection in vocal music came only when it was 'framed to the life of the words'—an expression which he used in his *Psalms, Songs, and Sonnets* of 1611.

The two books of *Cantiones Sacrae* demonstrate the great decline of the cantus firmus motet, of which there are only three examples (*Aspice Domine, Descendit de coelis,* and *Afflicti pro peccatis*), the remaining compositions being unified by an expressive and imitative contrapuntal style quite independent of plainsong influences. The *Gradualia,* whose two books constitute that great liturgical rarity—settings of the Proper for Feasts of the Virgin, and for Corpus Christi, All Saints, Christmas, Epiphany, Easter and Whitsun, together with the Feast of the Ascension and that of St. Peter and St. Paul—embody techniques which are even more restrained and refined, bearing out in musical sounds the thought which Byrd had expressed in his long dedication to Lord Northampton.[3] The part played by the texts in the inspiration of the music is rightly thrown into relief by Byrd, who found that meditation on the texts often caused the themes to suggest themselves spontaneously. In most instances the inspiration seems to have been of a general nature, reflecting the mood and sense of the text in so far as that is possible; yet on occasion Byrd has allowed himself to be affected by the word rather than by the phrase, and accordingly he describes the word in terms of pure music. These effects, seldom but always tastefully used, are for the ear rather than for the eye; they constitute word-sounding, not word-painting.

Music was often composed in Tudor times for special services and state occasions, and some of the motets belonging to this class have already been discussed. Paraliturgical motets are much more rare, for they do not form part of the liturgy, nor do their texts come from the Bible. For this reason the texts and the musical settings vary much more than other, more strictly liturgical genres.[4] *O bone Jesu,* which was set by Robert Carver, Robert Fayrfax, Robert Parsons, and one anonymous composer,

[1] *William Byrd: Complete Works,* ed. E. H. Fellowes, vols. II and III.
[2] *ibid,* IV–VII; also *Tudor Church Music,* VII.
[3] Reprinted in Strunk, *Source Readings in Music History,* p. 327.
[4] Many texts may be found in private devotional books; for example the *Stella celi* mentioned above (p. 36) occurs in Books of Hours written in the fifteenth and sixteenth centuries.

illustrates changes in length and internal structure caused by differences of textual disposition. The prayer consists fundamentally of a number of short petitions separated by acclamations similar to those which appear in *Salve regina*.[1] The anonymous setting begins 'O bone Jesu, O dulcis Jesu, O mitis Jesu'; Carver and Fayrfax diverge after the opening words to a series of superlatives—'O piissime Jesu, O dulcissime Jesu'. Fayrfax and anonymous agree about the ending, but Carver is far more expansive, and instead of finishing with *Amen* he adds several more petitions and another group of superlative acclamations: a fitting conclusion for a motet in nineteen real parts. The motet by Parsons is different entirely, for it makes use of a framework of psalm verses with interpolated acclamations such as 'O Adonay', 'O Heloy', 'O Emmanuel', 'O Raby'.[2]

Polyphonic settings of the Lamentations of Jeremiah varied only in the number of lessons composed: their structure was basically the same, and included harmonizations of the Hebrew letters preceding each section. Parsley's *Lamentations* alone make use of the chant: settings by Byrd,[3] John Mundy, Ferrabosco, White,[4] and Tallis[5] are in free contrapuntal style. Tallis's music is often spoilt by being sung at the wrong pitch. It was intended for male voices only, and the dark tone colour which results is entirely in keeping with the penitential character of the text. Both of White's settings

call for boys' voices, and achieve their solemnity and dignity more from the innate

---

[1] Certain of the phrases appear to have been taken from various parts of the *Festum dulcissimi nominis Jesu* (August 7). What is almost certainly a translation of part of *O bone Jesu* may be seen among the various 'Godly Prayers' of the Prayer Book of Queen Elizabeth.

[2] Oxford, Christ Church, Mss. 979–83; 984–88.

[3] *Tudor Church Music*, IX, p. 153.

[4] *idem*, V, pp. 14, 35.

[5] *idem*, VI, pp. 102, 110.

reverence of the counterpoint than from any unusual textural feature. Of two note-worthy polyphonic versions of the Passion according to St. Matthew, one is anony-mous, and was probably composed before the end of Henry's VIII's reign,[1] while the other (also for four voices) is earlier still. It is preserved in the Eton choirbook, and is unfortunately one of the incomplete works, but enough remains to show the skill and resources of its author, Richard Davy, who was at one time organist of Mag-dalen College, Oxford. He is the composer who is said to have written O *domine celi terreque* in the space of one day. If this statement (found in the Eton choirbook) is true, then Davy must have been endowed with the gift of speed as well as of great contrapuntal skill, for the work in question is scored for five-part choir and ranks among the longest motets in the manuscript.

A comparison of his motet *In honore summae Matris* with one by Byrd, *Non vos relinquam orphanos*, displays the great differences in style caused by the century of change and development which separated them. Davy's motet is in the Eton manuscript:[2] Byrd's is taken from the second book of *Gradualia*.[3] Both are five-part settings, and both have exactly the same adequate vocal range—22 notes, as the Eton designation expresses it. But there the resemblance ends. Discounting the obvious physical differ-ences between a setting of a lengthy hymn to the Virgin and a relatively short poly-phonic antiphon to the Magnificat, the contrasts of style are quite remarkable.

Davy evolves an ever-changing plan of remarkable complexity which serves pur-poses both useful and artistic. The greater part of his composition consists of duos and trios for various combinations of solo voices, not necessarily adjacent. Indeed, there are several instances of fairly long sections for soprano and tenor, or even soprano and bass, and it so happens that both of these duo-combinations (so often found in pre-Reformation vocal music) sound as effective in a large building as they look ineffec-tive on paper. Four-part harmony is almost non-existent, and five-part sections for full choir are carefully spaced out at first, then gradually closed up as the work reaches its climax. The dynamic build-up is natural and logical throughout, a duo leading to a trio, which in turn expands into a five-part section. Ample contrast results between few and many voices, and between high and low pitch, while the usefulness of the scheme lies in the lengthy rests for the voices not employed in the different trios and duos. No voice is made to sing for too long at a stretch, and the five voice-parts are split up into some fifteen separate combinations during the course of the work, thus exploiting to the full not only the range but the depth of vocal colour inherent in even a small choir. The counterpoint is largely non-imitative, in the best Franco-

[1] British Museum, Add. Ms. 17802–5.
[2] *The Eton Choirbook*, II, p. 105.
[3] *Tudor Church Music*, VII, p. 318.

Flemish tradition, and gains its impetus by the incessant weaving of flexible and volatile melodic patterns. Melismatic passages occur from time to time throughout

the entire work, but their extended use is restricted to the full sections, and of course the final Amen. The cantus firmus, *Justi in perpetuum vivent*, suggests a performance at Vespers on the Feast of Relics or of All Saints, both of which were classed as Greater Doubles in the Sarum Kalendar.

Byrd's antiphon is also designed to be sung at Vespers, but the feast (as shown by the text) is that of Pentecost. There is no cantus firmus, and no reliance on plainsong. Each significant phrase, or even word, is given its own clearly recognizable theme, whilst the word 'Alleluia' occurs continually in varying melodic garb, often forming counterpoint invertible at the fifth or octave with the other themes. At certain points 'Alleluia' appears as a refrain, until new themes and a new fragment of the text take over and run their course. Imitation is as a rule quite strict and usually very close, but the themes are chosen and contrived in such a way as to induce no waywardness or lack of balance into the harmonic scheme, which seems generally simple and unsophisticated. Rests are for the most part short, giving just sufficient time for the

singers to snatch a breath; the result is that the five-voice texture is practically continuous, although there is a certain sense of ebb and flow, of constant renewal of vocal and musical resources, which gives the work its drive and its noble sonority. Melismas occur, as indeed they should, on the closing 'Alleluia', and the spacing of the voices at the climax proves Byrd a consummate master of choral textures.

IV

Music for the English Rite

Fortunately for the Elizabethans, religious music set to English texts had almost as long a tradition as Latin church music, although the main difference between the two was in quantity. Thanks to the macaronic habits of carol-writers, English texts appear alongside Latin ones in nearly all the important manuscript sources, and if the contention that the carol was processional music has the support of scholars, it is not unreasonable to find in it the beginnings of vernacular polyphony.[1] The average Plantagenet carol is no more highly contrapuntal that the anthems and services composed during the first two decades of the reign of Elizabeth: it was the intervening period spanned by Henry VII and Henry VIII that saw the true zenith of Tudor polyphony, majestic to the point of extravagance, and sublimely indifferent to the audibility of the texts.

Even Tudor carols, with all their devotion to fashionable melismata, begin to show strong traces of a new, often dramatic outlook in the manner of setting words. Composers took great care that the text should be audible on its first appearance. Once enunciated—often with a syllable to a note—the phrase is allowed to merge into expressive vocalization; and the texture, from a lone utterance such as that which begins Cornyshe's *Woefully arrayed*,[2] (Ex. 17) becomes at once more dense and more motet-like. The earliest truly liturgical music for the English rite was composed towards the end of Henry VIII's reign, and although it lacks the striking solos and delectable duos of its immediate precursors, it has a unique character through being neither wholly chordal (like certain carols and para-liturgical works) nor completely contrapuntal in the way that some of Byrd's mature English anthems are.

The answer to those who maintain that late Henrician works are tentative and

---

[1] See in particular the mid-fifteenth century carols in *Musica Britannica*, IV (edited by John Stevens).

[2] British Museum Add. Ms. 5465 (the Fayrfax Manuscript) where the same text is also set by John Browne. Composers of other carols in this source are Sheryngham, Gilbert Banester, and Richard Davy.

unoriginal is not that their composers were intimidated by Cranmerian precepts, nor that they were the fruits of an imperfect technique. A composer of the standing of Tallis, who could fill the lofty vaults of Waltham Abbey with the massive sonority of a forty-part motet or a canonically intricate *Miserere*, would hardly boggle at a straightforward piece of four-part harmony, note-against-note in the main. One would expect a dignified composition, outwardly simple, yet full of cunning part-writing and careful spacing of voice-parts, breathing to a quiet rhythmic pulse by no means lacking in fine and subtle touches. This, indeed, is what often did result from these early experiments in harmonizing texts from Henry VIII's *Prymer* of 1545.[1] But apart from a few published examples, they are insufficiently well known, often because the absence of a single part-book has acted in some measure as a deterrent to inveterate transcribers.

It is frequently stated that the two halves of the sixteenth century were connected musically across the gulf which separated Elizabeth's broad Protestantism and Henry VIII's even broader Catholicism. This is only a half-truth, however, for the continuity that undoubtedly existed was a musico-technical one, and not musico-liturgical. The emphasis placed on this point is necessary in order to dispel the false but widespread idea that 'the motet corresponded to the anthem, and the Mass to the Service'. The term 'motet', as has already been shown, was loosely applied to polyphonic music for the choir office and the Proper of the Mass. The Elizabethan anthem, de-

---

[1] And, of course, from Marshall's *Goodly Prymer* of 1535, and Hilsey's *Manual of Prayers*, published in 1539. It is nevertheless clear from the texts of those canticles preserved in such manuscripts as British Museum Roy. App. 74–6, Add. Mss. 30480–4, and Harley 7578, that there were many intermediate stages in the evolution of the Prayer Book version, and some of these were used for musical settings. Frere points out that one of the three extant versions of *Venite* is quite unlike any of the Primers, and while it agrees in general with the Prayer Book version, there are still considerable points of divergence. For further details and lists of the contents of these part-books, see Frere, *Edwardine Vernacular Services before the First Prayer Book*, in *Alcuin Club Collections*, XXXV (1940), p. 5.

signed to follow the Third Collect at Morning and Evening Prayer 'in Quires and Places where they sing' was, as the Prayer Book tells us, by no means an essential part of the liturgy. It was a pleasant adornment to the ceremony, but one which could easily be dispensed with. The so-called 'motet' could not be dispensed with unless plainsong took its place. Similarly, the Mass and the Service no more correspond with each other than do the anthem and the motet. Composers in England usually set four sections of the Ordinary of the Mass; and after the Reformation, when it became imperative to write Services, a small but important group of these same composers found that their task included the setting to music of a wide variety of liturgical texts: Preces, Venite, Te Deum, Benedictus, Responses, Litany, Kyrie, Creed, Sanctus, Gloria, Magnificat and Nunc Dimittis.

The Service, then, in its fullest form, was a compound of choral music for the Communion, and for Morning and Evening Prayer; it cannot be said to derive from the Mass in any way, apart from the superficial act of translation from Latin into English.[1] The great majority of Elizabethan Services included only Kyrie and Creed as choral music for the Communion: of these the Kyrie was normally a choral version of the responses to the Ten Commandments, and not a tripartite structure as it had been in the Latin rite, or in the late Henrician English Masses. This change in the nature of the Kyrie took place at the same time as the removal of the Gloria to the end of the Communion, and was enforced by the Prayer Book of 1552. The extreme Protestantism of Edward VI's reign may have been partly responsible for the musical setting of only Kyrie and Creed, since the remaining sections (Sanctus and Benedictus, Agnus Dei, and Gloria) occurred during the latter and more solemn part of the Communion service, when music was probably frowned upon.[2]

It is noticeable that pre-Edwardian music for the Communion service, unlike the later Elizabethan settings, tended to include the entire number of texts whose choral performance was approved by tradition. This is certainly true of the Communion services in the Wanley part-books, which are usually dated 1546–47.[3] Of ten complete services, only three omit the Kyrie, and even then the remainder of the texts are set, and even amplified by harmonized versions of the Offertory Sentences or the Post-communion. More significant still is that one of these ten services, by Heath, was

---

[1] At the opening Mass of Parliament and Convocation on November 4, 1547, the *Gloria in excelsis, Credo*, and *Agnus Dei* were all sung in English. Six months later an augmented St. Paul's choir sang Mattins, Mass and Evensong in English. On May 12, 1548, the choir of Westminster Abbey sang in English the anniversary Mass of Henry VII. (Frere, *op. cit.*, p. 7).

[2] There was a century or more of tradition behind this apparently unusual state of affairs. Even in the compositions of the Old Hall Manuscript, which show considerable French influence, there is a noticeable division of style between the often complex settings of *Gloria* and *Credo*, and the comparatively simple polyphony of the non-isorhythmic *Sanctus* and *Agnus* settings.

[3] Oxford, Bodleian Library, Ms. Mus. Sch. E 420–422.

printed by Day in *Certaine Notes . . . to be sung at the Mornyng Communion* (1560), but without Benedictus and Agnus Dei. In similar fashion the greatest of the Elizabethan Communion settings, including those by Byrd (both the Short and Great Services) and by Richard Farrant and Thomas Morley, contain only Kyrie and Creed.[1]

Notable exceptions to this procedure are the two best-known settings by Tallis. The so-called Dorian Service has a predominantly syllabic, though occasionally florid texture.[2] Such florid passages as do occur are mostly confined to the inner parts at cadences. The part-writing however is of a highly competent order, both effective and sonorous within its limits. There is even a hint, in certain sections, of a head-motive— a mere four-note group—which may indicate that Tallis tried to retain some vestige of the cyclic form prevalent in his Latin music. It is to the credit of Tallis that he avoids monotony in spite of his epigrammatic, chant-like treatment of the individual items, and the chordal nature of the harmonization. At least two other services of his must at one time have existed in complete form: the bass part of one (preserved in the library of St. John's College, Oxford) proves that it was a full Service of very considerable proportions. The indication 'of five parts, two in one' implies, moreover, that two of the parts were in canon for most if not all of the time. An English Te Deum, also of five parts (see Ex. 18, p. 54), almost certainly comes from another Service which would have included music for the Communion.[3]

Farrant's Service,[4] as already mentioned, contains only two sections of the Communion: Kyrie and Creed. They echo certain of Tallis's stylistic features, and (like his music) could perfectly well be sung by men, since the uppermost part never exceeds counter-tenor range. Byrd's Short Service breaks new ground by lightening the texture and contrasting various combinations of voice-parts. There are, it is true, paired entries from time to time in Farrant's Service, but the idea of contrast in texture is carried no further than this. With Byrd the procedure is fairly complex, and results in a welcome enlargement of expressive qualities and in effectual dynamic range. The Creed, as set by Byrd, even extends certain delicate hints (already apparent in Tallis and Farrant) of word-painting, especially at the phrases *And the third day He rose again*

[1] Essential for a thorough study of the services and anthems of this period is the collection published in 1641 by John Barnard (a minor canon of St. Paul's Cathedral) called *The First Book of Selected Church Musick*. The separate part-books were transcribed into score by John Bishop, and although this gigantic task was completed in 1876 with a view to publication, nothing came of the project. Bishop's scores are now in the British Museum (Add. Mss. 30085-87). The original transcriptions made by Barnard (including numerous works not included in his 1641 publication) may also be consulted (RCM Mss. 1045-51).

[2] It should be noted that the reprint of this work in Boyce's *Cathedral Music*, 1760-78; 1788; 1844 (Vincent Novello); 1849 (Joseph Warren) substitutes an anonymous chant known as 'The Christ Church Tune' for Tallis's Venite.

[3] Reconstructed by E. H. Fellowes and published as no. 72 of the Tudor Church Music Octavo Series.

[4] The Morning and Evening Canticles are available in the TCM Octavo Series, nos. 62 and 33. Boyce's transcriptions are not completely reliable.

Ex.18   TALLIS

... *and ascended into heaven*. Comparable treatment of this portion of the text may be seen in the Great Service, which makes the fullest use of antiphonal effects.[1]

[1] Byrd's four Services have been reprinted in *Tudor Church Music*, II, also in Fellowes's edition of the complete works of Byrd, X.

Antiphonal singing was not always appreciated during the early part of Elizabeth's reign, and the complex structure of the verse anthem which came into vogue well before the end of the sixteenth century can have done little to assuage the wrath of the Puritans, for whom it was a wilful continuation of pre-Reformation practices. A London clergyman named John Field even went so far as to write 'An Admonition to the Parliament' in 1572, criticizing the Anglican Service where 'there is no edification, according to the Rule of the Apostle, but confusion; they tosse the Psalmes in most places like tennice-balls'. Edward Hake, writing in Daman's *Psalmes of David* (1579) talks with equal feeling of the 'over curious, yea, and as I may say over tragicall dismembring not onely of wordes but of letters and sillables in the holy Psalmes and Anthemes appointed to the praysing of God'. If all this were true of Psalm settings, it must have been equally true of music for the Communion service as sung in Cathedrals and the Chapel Royal, designated as 'popyshe dennes' and 'patternes . . . of all superstition' in the tract written by Field. Fortunately for the Anglican Church there were men of the calibre and integrity of John Case, who replied to these detractors by emphasizing the place which antiphonal singing held in the earliest days of the Christian Church, as well as in ancient Jewish ritual.[1] There is, moreover, no clear evidence that those who criticized the Anglican way of singing had any sound alternative to offer. John Marbeck's *Booke of Common Praier Noted*, published in 1550, had failed to arouse any enthusiasm, although its quasi-mensural notation of unison chant should have satisfied the most ardent among reformers. It may well have been that its superficial resemblance to plainsong counted against its formal adoption by the adherents of four-part harmony and strict homophony. It is nevertheless interesting to compare the rhythmical schemes adopted by Marbeck in his setting of the Creed with exactly similar passages in Tallis's Dorian Service. There are enough coincidences to suggest that Tallis must have known Marbeck's music even before it came to be printed.[2]

The canticles for Morning and Evening Service were less subject to change than the component parts of the Communion service, and a composer working on English texts from 1545 onwards would have had only changes of translation and phraseology to contend with, instead of the fluctuating list of items in the Communion service, and the attendant confusion over what to include and what not to include. The grouping of Magnificat and Nunc Dimittis is found five times in the Wanley manuscripts, and besides these there is one separate and apparently unattached setting of Magnificat. Of the four groupings of morning canticles (Te Deum and Bene-

---

[1] *The Praise of Musicke* (1586).

[2] See the Appendix to *The Office of the Holy Communion as set by John Merbecke*, ed. E. H. Fellowes (1949).

dictus) two have a Venite also; and once again there is a separate Venite which, like the Magnificat, appears not to belong to any of the other groups. One of the sets of evening canticles is probably the work of Tye (the Nunc Dimittis is attributed to him in another, and fortunately complete set of part-books[1]) who with Tallis was among the first to attempt an intelligent solution of the problems posed by the Anglican liturgy. Another evening service formerly attributed to Tye is now known to be the work of Osbert Parsley, sometime lay-clerk of Norwich Cathedral.[2] Byrd, whose Short and Great Services have done so much to enhance his reputation, left two sets of evening canticles which deserve to be better known. One is an early pioneer of the Verse Service, with passages for solo voice accompanied by the organ; the other, largely in compound duple time, contains subtle harmonic colours and an ingenious use of canon.

Ex.19   BYRD — THIRD SERVICE

Melodic links between Magnificat and Nunc Dimittis were not frequent in Elizabethan settings, although there is a slight resemblance between the opening of the two canticles in Byrd's Short Service, and a definite duplication of material in Farrant's Benedictus and Nunc Dimittis. If thematic connections between the music for Morning and Evening Prayer seems extraordinary, similar links between great Elizabethan composers in their different versions of the Te Deum must be accepted as an artistic commonplace. The most interesting example of this is to be found in the melodic material used for the words *Holy, Holy, Holy, Lord God of Sabaoth*. Byrd,

[1] British Museum Add. Mss. 30480–84.
[2] The 'Gloria Patri' of Parsley's Benedictus (*Tudor Church Music*, X, p. 271) corresponds to that of the Nunc Dimittis in his Evening Service (*ibid.*, p. 293). A similar concordance of musical material in Farrant's Service is mentioned above.

Farrant, Tallis and Bevin make use of exactly the same phrase for these words: a descending scale-segment of four notes, falling from the mediant to the leading-note of a minor scale.

Most composers naturally made the best possible use of tonal contrasts resulting from the subdivision of the choir. Those singing on the side of the Dean's stall (Decani) were thus able to answer or join with an equivalent group on the north side (Cantoris) so called because of the Precentor's stall. It must be stressed that this English practice was in no way reliant upon the traditions of polychoralism, whose most important function apart from antiphony was the creation of a richer texture when the two choirs combined. Decani and Cantoris sides both consisted of S.A.T.B. groups which, when they coincided, usually sang exactly the same notes, resulting in an increase of volume rather than an increase in the density of the polyphonic texture.[1] The introduction of verses for soloists, however, gave innumerable opportunities for complex and subtle interchanges of register, timbre, and volume; and it was due to the development of this technique by Byrd and Morley that the most prolific of Elizabethan composers of Services, Thomas Weelkes, came to contrive his magnificent evening canticles for seven voices. Four altos are needed for the performance of this work, which has survived in a form complete enough for a reconstruction to be made. In richness and resource it is perhaps without parallel in the whole of the Elizabethan repertory, for Weelkes's ingenuity in marshalling his kaleidoscopic verse sections is matched only by the seven-part writing of the full sections.

At least nine other Services by Weelkes are known to exist in fairly complete form, and they range from a normal four-part setting of 'Short Service' stature to Verse Services of generous proportions and fine workmanship. Tomkins, whose work (like that of Gibbons) is really outside the scope of this survey, wrote at least seven Services, most of them being of the Verse type.[2] Gibbons's Verse Service is sometimes thought to be less convincing musically than his Short Service, which is one of his best-known and most frequently sung compositions. Of Shepherd's three Services, only one—fortunately an excellent and vigorous specimen—is complete.[3] It proves that its author, like his contemporary, Tallis, was in no way restricted by the insistence on simplicity in liturgical music: indeed, it seems rather to have acted as a spur in the

[1] The Benedicite in the incomplete set of Henrician part-books, Roy. App. 74–6, is set out quite clearly for two alternating choirs. This manner of performance may have been intended in other instances where indications for *alternatim* performance are not specifically given. See the Scottish version of Te Deum by Andro Kemp, in *Musica Britannica*, XV, p. 128. This volume also contains music by John Angus, Andro Blackhall, and David Peebles, for use in the services of the reformed church.

[2] The works by Gibbons are discussed in E. H. Fellowes, *Orlando Gibbons and His Family*; those by Tomkins in Denis Stevens, *Thomas Tomkins, 1572–1656*.

[3] See the manuscript collection made by John Barnard prior to the publication of his *First Book of Selected Church Musick* (RCM Mss. 1045–51).

creation of a fresh and clarified polyphonic outlook. This outlook was certainly shared by William Mundy and Robert Parsons in their Services, while the work of lesser figures such as Nathaniel Patrick, John Amner, John Holmes and Nathaniel Giles affords ready proof of a widespread respect for this new and healthy musical texture, with its fine balance between counterpoint and homophony.

It is often difficult to realize that alongside this intensive pursuit of church music for its own sake (for there were no outlets worth speaking of in the world of printing and publishing) the choirs were often badly looked after, meagrely rewarded for their services, and much reduced in numbers. The economic position in England had steadily deteriorated throughout the reign of Henry VIII, and its effect on musical establishments is only too readily apparent in contemporary allusions to choirs. In Roger Ascham's *Toxophilus* (1545) one of the characters, or rather interlocutors, bewails the unhappy state of musical education, wishing 'that the laudable custom of England to teach children their pricksong, were not so decayed throughout all the realm as it is'. Twenty years later the position was still as bad, if we are to believe the retrospective musings of an anonymous seventeenth-century writer on church music.[1] It is his contention that 'the first occasion of the decay of Musick in Cathedrall Churches and other places, where musick and singing was used and had yearly allowance began about the ninth yeare of Queene Elizabeth'.

The fact was that retrenchments of one kind or another—not only in the 'yearly allowance'—had been taking place steadily through the troubled reigns of Edward and Mary, and the damage done to the structure of cathedral music was serious enough to create a continuing weakness in what should have been a strong national tradition. One method of making ends meet involved the reduction of numbers in

[1] British Museum Roy. 18 B xix (*The praise of musick, the profite and delight it bringeth to man & other the creatures of God, and the necessarye use of it in the service & Christian Churche of God*).

the choir, so that the fixed amount of money available could be divided among fewer people. Another method was to import men from the city to the cathedral at a low salary, as at Canterbury in 1560, where the statutory number of twelve minor canons could not otherwise be maintained.[1] The organist or master of the children was often hard hit by economic difficulties, for more often than not he had to provide for the children's board and lodging as well as teach them daily. In 1583, William Hunnis, then Master of the Children of the Chapel Royal, petitioned for an increase in allowances, which was not apparently granted. Complaining of the difference between 'the prices of things present to the time past' he says: 'the burden hereof hath from time to time so hindered the masters of the children, viz. Master Bower, Master Edwardes, myself and Master Farrant: that notwithstanding some good helps otherwise some of them died in so poor a case, and so deeply indebted that they have not left scarcely wherewith to bury them'.[2] Yet there was good spirit among the community of musicians as a whole. They struggled gallantly to maintain what was, to them, a worthwhile tradition of composition and performance; and their music, having little or no commercial value—unlike its continental counterpart—was a means to a spiritual end. 'The better the voice is', said William Byrd, 'the meeter it is to honour and serve God therewith: and the voice of man is chiefly to be employed to that end.'[3]

The new liturgical reforms, however, were concerned not only with the voice of man but the voice of many: the sharing in certain parts of the service, notably the psalms, which any musical congregation might be expected to approve. Music was slow, at first, to appear in the many published psalters, and the harmonizations were understandably functional rather than artistic—an attribute which remained throughout the succeeding centuries, and which caused the eminent Bohemian composer, Dvořák, to ask why the choir of St. Paul's Cathedral persisted in repeating a bad tune so often. Oddly enough, some of the best Tudor psalm-tunes, those written by Thomas Tallis for Archbishop Parker's Psalter, were never circulated in their own time, since the Psalter was printed but never placed on sale.[4] The composers of the tunes in Sternhold and Hopkins's Psalter of 1562 are unknown; but the thirty additional tunes given in the Day Psalter, published in the following year, were the work of men such as Thomas Caustun and William Parsons. Psalmody during the last two decades of the century received further stimulus from varied publications by Allison, Byrd, Cosyn, Daman, Denham, and East. East's *Whole Booke of Psalmes* (1592) contains settings by ten or more composers; Allison's *Psalmes of David in Metre*, however,

[1] Woodfill, *Musicians in English Society*, p. 136.
[2] Chambers, *The Elizabethan Stage*, II, p. 37.
[3] *Psalms, sonets, and songs of sadnes and pietie* (1588).
[4] They are reprinted in M. C. Boyd, *Elizabethan Music and Musical Criticism*, pp. 45–52; also in the article by Leonard Ellinwood, *Tallis' Tunes and Tudor Psalmody*, in *Musica Disciplina*, II (1948), p. 189.

consists entirely of his own work.[1] A few composers, notably Tallis, Byrd, Morley, and Gibbons, set parts of psalms for special festivals in a manner which was akin to chanting, yet more florid and interesting than straightforward chants. These versions were given the name of *Psalmi Festivales*, a term which was wide enough to include even a rudimentary 'Verse Anthem' type such as Byrd's *Teach me O Lord*, set out for full choir alternating with solo voice and organ.[2]

Psalm texts were, of course, greatly in demand for anthems of all types. Byrd included ten five-part Psalms in his publication *Psalms, Sonets and Songs* (1588), and may have been responsible for the English adaptation of *Attollite portas*, from *Cantiones Sacrae* of 1575, which became widely known as *Lift up your heads*. It is not always possible to attribute arrangements and adaptations to the original composer, even if it is assumed that his approval would have extended so far. Yet many anthems current in Elizabethan times were direct arrangements of motets. Some even inspired two separate texts: Taverner's *In nomine* (not really a motet, but part of his Mass *Gloria tibi Trinitas*) provided the musical structure for an anthem, published in Day's *Certaine notes* . . . (1560). The text of this version was *In trouble and adversitie*, whereas a

Ex.21   TAVERNER — IN NOMINE

contemporary manuscript using the same music has an English setting which begins *O give thanks unto the Lord*.[3] Two well-known anthems by Tallis, *O sacred and holy banquet* and *I call and cry*, are both adapted from *O sacrum convivium*, and the same composer's *Absterge Domine* gave rise to two anthems (*Wipe away my sins* and *Discumfit them O Lord*) the latter having been often, though in error, associated with the defeat of the Spanish Armada. In both cases it will be noticed that one of

[1] Allison's harmonization of 'Winchester' is printed in Boyd, *op. cit.*, p. 55. East's publication was edited by Rimbault for the *Musical Antiquarian Society*, XI.

[2] *Tudor Church Music*, II, p. 30; also *Byrd, Complete Works*, X, p. 46.

[3] British Museum, Add. Mss. 30480–84.

the texts bears some relation to the Latin original: the other is quite separate and unrelated. Later editors and collectors, including Aldrich, Boyce, and Oliphant, made numerous adaptations of motets; but having grafted on an English text they often disposed of the Latin one so completely that an accurate reference is a matter of some difficulty. The close connection between psalm and motet may be seen in the versions of Tallis's *O Lord in Thee is all my trust* and *Remember not O Lord God* as they appear in Day's *Certaine notes*, and in *The Whole Psalmes* which followed three years later. In both cases the second version is much abridged.

Day was the first English publisher of anthems, and although his books must have served the public well, there was no comparison between the cost of copying an anthem by hand, and the cost of publication. Consequently there were few successors to Day's venture in the field of liturgical music until long after the close of Elizabeth's reign. Byrd's collections of vocal and instrumental pieces contained secular items in addition to psalms and works with sacred texts, while the *Teares or Lamentacions of a Sorrowfull Soule*, published in 1614 by Sir William Leighton, had exclusively religious texts but a pointedly secular style of instrumentation.[1] The majority of late Tudor anthems are therefore preserved at first hand in manuscript sources only, and did not reach the printing-press until John Barnard's *First Book of Selected Church Musick* (1641).

The earliest type of full anthem was never so called: the term 'full' was introduced at a later date in contrast to 'verse'. Nor indeed was the full anthem invariably written throughout for full choir. The normal division of Decani and Cantoris sides of the choir resulted in antiphonal singing in anthems as well as Services, so that for the greater part of the time the full strength of the choir was not being used. A few modern editions still fail to take this antiphonal practice into account, even when it is most explicit in the music itself. Tye's four-part *I will exalt Thee*[2] is a case in point. Both Tye and Shepherd left a small but distinguished collection of anthems, of which fourteen from each composer have come down to us. Of Tallis's work, seventeen anthems are now recoverable. Some of these, for example, *If ye love me*, are to be sung antiphonally; others like *Purge me O Lord* are straightforward 'full' settings, varying from quasi-syllabic works to contrapuntal structures of considerable elaboration.[3]

There are numerous liturgical anthems by Okeland, Caustun, Johnson, Shepherd and Whitbroke in the Wanley manuscripts and in sources contemporary with them, and it is much to be regretted that these unique early sources are often incomplete.

---

[1] No less than seventeen of these compositions have accompaniments provided for lute, bandora, and cittern, thus presupposing domestic performance in the same tradition as Tye's *Acts of the Apostles*.

[2] TCM Octavo Series, no. 59.

[3] *idem*, nos. 69 and 67. A useful list of reprints and revisions of Tye's music for the *Acts of the Apostles* may be seen in Brennecke, *John Milton the Elder*, p. 19.

Concordances increase in later Tudor times, with the result that a fair number of anthems by Parsons, Byrd, Farrant, White and their fellow-composers is recoverable, thereby illuminating the high degree of technical equipment possessed by the best men of the Elizabethan school of church musicians. The later group, including not

only Weelkes, Gibbons and Tomkins, but also Byrd (who lived on until 1623) were all enthusiastic supporters of the Verse Anthem, although it is often hinted that their compositions in this vein cannot bear comparison with their other works. The 'verses', so named perhaps after the verses of psalms which had originally been used for texts, gave soloists an opportunity to shine, and the number of solo voices needed would vary from one to six, occasionally even more. Verses were accompanied on the organ, and parts for this instrument were often sketched out for the use of the player. If no organ were to hand, viols could be (and often were) used to good effect, especially in anthems suitable for performance in a private chapel (Ex. 22).[1]

There is no doubt that the musical vigour of the anthem, as an art-form, had few rivals in Elizabethan times. It retained that vigour until the death of Purcell, but its highest peaks were topped well before the end of James I's reign.

[1] See Arkwright, *Note on the instrumental accompaniment of church music in the sixteenth and early seventeenth centuries*, in *John Milton: Six Anthems*.

V

The Role played by Instruments

It would be a great error to think of Tudor church music as an exclusively vocal culture, even though the form in which it is usually made available—either as printed text or as actual sound—pays scant regard to instrumental participation. There is no doubt that at certain times during the Tudor epoch, instruments played an important role in music performed in cathedrals, college chapels, and of course the Chapel Royal. At other times, notably those years when reforming zeal was at its height, there was a grave danger that even that most hallowed of all ecclesiastical instruments, the organ, would be for ever banished and silenced. Fortunately the danger was averted, and both organs and organists suffered less than they did in the time of the Commonwealth. But the official outlook, as expressed in the second *Tome of Homelyes*, published in 1563 and appointed 'to be read in eurey paryshe Churche agreablye', referred to the piping, singing, chanting and playing upon the organs as 'things which displeased God so sore, and filthily defiled his holy house and place of prayer'.[1] Extreme views of this kind did not however go unchallenged, thanks to the existence of a small but influential group of reasonable persons in the universities and cathedral cities. One such person, John Case of Oxford, published an elaborate and plausible defence of church music in *The Praise of Musicke* (1586) where he is careful to emphasize biblical traditions.[2]

'But the holy Ghost, the author of the Psalms, appointed and commanded them by the prophet *David*, to be song, and to be song most cunningly, and to be song with diverse artificiall instruments of Musick, and to be song with sundry, severall, and most excellent notes and tunes.' Case concludes that the English church is completely justified in thus performing the psalms. Commenting a few pages later on

[1] Homily of the Place and Time of Prayer (part 2).
[2] Thomas Watson's poem in honour of Case, *Let others praise what seems them best*, was set to music by William Byrd and published, but only one page is now known to exist.

the attitude towards organ playing, he voices his disapproval of the men who 'at the reading of the chapters should walke in the bodie of the church, and when the Orgaun play, give attentive heed thereunto: as if the whole and better part of service did consist in Musick'. That Case was able to make such a reservation proves that musical awareness had progressed considerably in a fairly short time, for less than twenty years before his book was published an exactly opposite attitude was rife: 'few or none of the people would vouchsafe to come into the Quyres during the singinge service but would stand without, dauncinge and sportinge themselves until the sermons and lectures did begin, scorning and derydinge both the service and those which were imployed therein. . . .'[1]

Before considering in detail the place of the organ in pre- and post-Reformation liturgies, it is significant to note the frequent incursions of other instruments, from the time of the *cantus firmus* Mass and motet to the beginnings of the verse anthem. There are unfortunately few early English pictorial proofs of the familiar scene of singers and players gathered around a large choirbook, supported on a lectern, although there are many continental examples.[2] Illuminations and engravings generally show such instruments as the cornett and the slide trumpet, these two instruments between them having the three-octave compass required by full-scale motets and Masses. The lack of illustrations in England is to some extent remedied by royal and capitular accounts which frequently mention players of the cornett or the sackbut.[3] Many of these players were full members of the musical establishment, and were held to be so important that on one occasion the income from a certain benefice was even diverted so that the cathedral could continue to enjoy its wind instrumentalists. When ingenious devices like this were either impossible or inadvisable, musicians were hired for special occasions from the town waits—skilled groups of players whose primary function as guardians and watchmen of the municipality was slowly being replaced by a new role concerned with official entertainments.

The tone of the cornett, when well played, was said to resemble very nearly the timbre of the human voice:[4] thus it was an ideal instrument for the accompaniment

---

[1] British Museum, Roy. 18 B xix.

[2] See, for example, the illustration from Hermann Finck's *Practica Musica* (1556) in Robert Haas, *Aufführungspraxis der Musik*, p. 125; or from the *Encomium Musices* of Gallaeus and Stradanus (1595) in *Musik und Bild: Festschrift Max Seiffert zum siebzigsten Geburtstag*, plate 19.

[3] References to Canterbury in 1532 and Worcester in 1575 are given in Woodfill, *Musicians in English Society*, p. 149.

[4] This is still confirmed as late as the early eighteenth century by the Hon. Roger North, who asks (concerning 'some other circumstances of former times') 'Is it not unlikely that organs and voices were not found in all or many great churches, as they are in most now, and what can yeild a tone so like an eunuch's voice as a true cornet pipe? In the north, where good or at least skillfull voices were scarce, and I am sure at Durham and Carlisle if not at York, the Quires in time of memory have had wind musick, to supply the want of voices, and sound great.' *Roger North on Music* (ed. John Wilson), p. 286.

or doubling of choral forces. Similarly, the slide trumpet (or sackbut, as it was called) gave excellent results in the hands of a skilled performer, and its considerable agility combined with possibilities of fine intonation and expert blend made it an admirable partner for the cornett. In addition, it was a tower of strength in the sustaining of long tenor *cantus firmi*, for although these were often conventionally underlaid with words, their long notes and even longer phrases marked them out as material for playing rather than for singing. Tenors of this type, in the early part of the fifteenth century, were often split up between two similar instruments, in order to give the players time to take in a fresh breath: *tenor* and *contratenor* would thus be complementary.[1] A conflate of these two, called *solus tenor*, was usually written down as a safeguard, and this had no breathing spaces at all, unless of course the isorhythmic pattern made allowance for them. The continuous nature of the *solus tenor* indicates the use of the organ, and we may therefore assume that two methods existed for performance of Mass sections and motets: one with organ alone, and the other with a consort of instruments. By the last two decades of the fifteenth century the accompanimental role of the large organ was gradually overshadowed by the new and rising star of the positive organ,[2] destined to become the chosen instrument of virtuosi. The steady development of organ technique was soon to equip it for a new and important role in the liturgy. But the other wind instruments remained, much to the annoyance of the purists, and it is no surprise to hear of Erasmus complaining about 'horns, trumpets and pipes constantly accompanying and alternating with the voices'. This is just the kind of performance commented upon by the Italian visitor mentioned in an earlier chapter,[3] and it was probably very fashionable up to 1525 or 1530, when the Tudor organists began to exploit their newly-coined techniques of elaborating plainsong.

During Elizabeth's reign, the pendulum swung back once more in favour of wind instruments, which we find accompanying the Queen on her royal visits to Worcester and Oxford. The Oxford visit took place in 1566, and a commendably careful observer tells us that the Queen 'entered into the church, and there abode, while the

---

[1] Compare the two Gloria settings by Pycard at pp. 84 and 92 of *The Old Hall Manuscript*, vol. I. The first (whose uppermost voice should proceed in canon at the sixth bar) is in five parts if both tenor and contratenor are used, but in four parts if these are replaced by the solus tenor; the second Gloria appears to be in six parts, but is actually in four, whether contratenor and tenor are used together, or whether they are replaced by solus tenor. The reason for this is that contratenor and tenor consist of only one melodic line, which is divided between two instruments.

[2] A positive is depicted in the triptych at Holyrood House, Edinburgh, formerly the property of the Collegiate Church of the Holy Trinity, whose first provost, Sir Edward Bonkil, is the central figure. A manuscript of the fifteenth century is open, appropriately enough, at *O lux beata Trinitas*, and the player is presumably about to provide an improvised descant to the plainsong. See the reproduction as frontispiece of Farmer, *A History of Music in Scotland*.

[3] See p. 22.

quyer sang and play'd with cornetts *Te Deum*'.[1] The next year, at Ely, we find an early reference to the teaching of the viol, which suggests that choristers were then beginning to learn an instrument which was something of a novelty to them:[2] yet this same instrument was destined to be accepted as the finest type of accompaniment for the verse anthem, so that the long supremacy of wind instruments was at last threatened, though never completely shaken.

The supremacy of the organ, and indeed of organ music, dates from the middle of Henry VIII's reign and extends to 1547, the year in which John Redford died.[3] From there onwards, it is connected by various subterranean streams to the vast output of Thomas Tomkins, who probably began his compilation of organ books—most of which are now lost—towards the very end of Elizabeth's reign. There is no evidence that organ music was published in England at any time during the period under review: everything composed was written down and passed on in manuscript form, much of which must have been lost or destroyed. In the history of organ music under the Tudors, there is a certain feeling of continuity rather akin to that which was apparent in their choral music. The link, in this instance, is the Offertory; the one point in the Mass or Communion Service where the organist could indulge his flights of fancy or improvisation. One of the earliest among many offertory settings still in existence is the *Felix namque* in a fifteenth-century manuscript in the Bodleian library.[4] This short, two-part composition, based on a Bridgettine variant of the familiar *Felix namque* plainsong, shows inventive and decorative faculties at work in a simple yet effective way. When, at the other extreme of the Tudor dynasty, we find references to Dr. Bull 'at the organ playing the Offertory' during an Easter Communion Service at court,[5] it is tempting to think that a similar plainsong was being used for the same purpose well over a hundred years later than the Bodleian fragment.

The organ offertory shows, perhaps more clearly than any other musico-liturgical form, the precise impact of the Reformation on Tudor composers. The earliest custom demanded that the priest or celebrant should intone the opening of the Offertory, just as in a monophonic choral interpretation.[6] But at the point where the chorus would normally enter, the organ began to play, and still keeping to the plainsong (or a variant

---

[1] *A brief rehearsall of all such things as were done in the University of Oxford during the Queen's Majesty's abode there* . . . by Richard Stephens (B.M. Harley Ms. 7033).

[2] This was in 1567. For further details see the article by Arkwright mentioned on p. 63.

[3] Even monastic houses were permitted by Wolsey to celebrate Masses of the Blessed Virgin, or of the Name of Jesus, with polyphonic singing and organs. (Wilkins, *Concilia Magnae Britanniae*, III, p. 686.)

[4] An account of this fragment, with a transcription, is given by Dart, *A New Source of Early English Organ Music*, in *Music and Letters*, XXXV (1954), p. 201.

[5] Rimbault, *The Old Cheque Book . . . of the Chapel Royal*, p. 150.

[6] *Exsultabunt sancti* (Thorne), *Letamini in Domino* (Coxsun), *Felix namque* (Preston) and an anonymous *Felix namque* are printed in *Altenglische Orgelmusik* (Bärenreiter; in England, Novello & Co. Ltd.).

at one remove, such as a faburden) embellished it with a constantly changing pattern of counterpoint and imitation. Settings by Redford (*Precatus est Moyses, Justus ut palma, Felix namque*), John Thorne of York (*Exsultabunt sancti*), Thomas Preston of St. George's, Windsor (*Reges Tharsis, Diffusa est gratia, Felix namque*) all show these

same features. Yet both Preston and Philip ap Rhys (who like Redford was an organist at St. Paul's Cathedral) wrote irregular settings of offertories, in which the priest's intonation is also set for the organ. This treatment foreshadows the post-Reformation settings by Tallis of *Felix namque*, where the intonation is not only set but even repeated.[1]

The mention of the term *faburden* calls for a detailed explanation because of its wide use among the Tudor organists, and also because the technique of composition to which it refers is often misunderstood.[2] The method of producing a faburden to a given plainsong was fundamentally quite simple and straightforward: a part, moving note against note with the plainsong, was written below it at the distance of a sixth or an octave. For obvious reasons sixths predominated, but octave intervals were generally used at the opening and close, and occasionally during the course of the piece; this prefabricated duet constituted, in effect, the skeleton of a regular faux-bourdon, as it would have been composed for vocal performance. But at this point there is a divergence in method. Where the composer of a choral fauxbourdon would add an extra part moving a perfect fourth below the plainsong, thus creating chains of $\frac{6}{3}$ chords, the organist would do away entirely with the original plainsong, retaining only the faburden. This he would use as both bass and basis of his contrapuntal superstructure (see Ex. 24).

The reason for doing this rather than using the original melody may be seen in the slightly more angular, functional-bass patterns of the faburden. Its harmonic implications were stronger than those of the plainsong, and it was thus peculiarly fitted to

---

[1] As in the first setting in the Fitzwilliam Virginal Book (vol. I, p. 427 of the Breitkopf edition).

[2] The term itself has still not been satisfactorily defined, nor has its morphological ancestry been completely uncovered, in spite of a number of articles devoted to it in *Acta Musicologica* between 1951 and 1954. See, for more recent discussions, Heinrich Besseler, *Das Ergebnis der Diskussion über 'Fauxbourdon'*, in *Acta*, XXIX (1957), p. 185; Sylvia Kenney, '*English Discant' and Discant in England*, in *The Musical Quarterly*, XLV (1959), p. 26; Brian Trowell, *Faburden and Fauxbourdon*, in *Musica Disciplina*, XIII (1959), p. 43.

be used as a cantus firmus in the bass. Later generations of organists occasionally moved it into the treble register—Blitheman does so in his *Te Deum*[1]—but this is a comparatively rare procedure. The title 'upon the faburden' is sometimes present as an appendage to the title of the plainsong itself, but its omission does not indicate that the music has not been based on a faburden.

It will be recalled that Erasmus, in his complaint about instrumental music in church, mentioned the alternation of instruments with voices. This age-old principle of antiphony lies at the root of nearly all the surviving organ music from Henry VIII's reign. In very few cases is the music complete on its own: it must always be arranged so that intervening verses can be sung in unison by a choir, either of men's voices alone, or of boys and men singing in octaves. Only then does the pattern of hymn, Magnificat, Mass, and Te Deum become clear to the modern listener.

Hymn verses are found in great profusion in the Tudor organist's repertoire. They outnumber by far even the great number of settings of the antiphon *Miserere mihi Domine*. The largest collection of hymn verses is to be found in a manuscript dating from Redford's time:[2] indeed there are many of his compositions in it, although it is no longer thought that some of the music is in his own handwriting. A hymn like *Salvator mundi Domine*, which usually has five verses, is given three organ verses in this manuscript, the inference being that the organist played verses 1, 3, and 5, and the choir sang verses 2 and 4. *Christe qui lux*, which has seven verses in all, has an organ version with four verses, presumably 1, 3, 5 and 7. The melody would always be present in the organ setting, although it was not exactly recognizable. Faburden might cover up its familiar contour, or (retaining its original shape) it might be absorbed into the texture by subtle and remarkable decoration. Then again, it might

---

[1] *The Mulliner Book* (*Musica Britannica*, I), p. 55.
[2] British Museum Add. Ms. 29996.

disappear from the aural perspective by clinging to one of the inner parts, as in the last three verses of Redford's *Christe qui lux*.[1] Only very exceptionally did the melody rise to the treble voice-part, although it does so proudly in the last verse of Blitheman's *Eterne rerum conditor*.[2] At the beginning of an important, though anonymous collection of hymns ranged in the order of the Christian year, Thomas Tomkins (a former owner of this same manuscript) has written 'all these are uppon the faburden of these playnsongs'. There are twenty complete hymns, ranging from *Conditor alme siderum* (Advent) as far as *Audi benigne conditor*, a Lenten hymn, as is the unfinished twenty-first piece *Ecce tempus idoneum*. All these show a mature and meticulous outlook on problems of setting plainsong, and in many the results are so fine that, to quote Morley, 'one not very well skilled in music should scant discern any plainsong at all.'[3]

Ex.25   ANON: LUCIS CREATOR OPTIME

Antiphons were less frequently taken by the organists, although there are two noble settings of *Lucem tuam*[4] (the antiphon to *Nunc Dimittis* at Compline in the feast of the Holy Trinity), one by Redford, and the other by Richard Winslade, who was organist of Winchester Cathedral in the early part of the sixteenth century. The two versions of *Glorificamus te Dei genitrix* are both anonymous, but they may well be the work of John Redford, whose fine four-part elaboration of this plainsong[5] shows his particular regard for its florid yet solemn character. The great number of *Miserere* settings is explained by the fact that this antiphon was so often used at Compline. A Sarum rubric enjoins the singing of the antiphon upon the Compline psalms 'throughout Advent, and from the morrow of the Octave of the Epiphany to Quadragesima, and from Sunday in the Passion of the Lord up to the Supper of The Lord, and from the morrow of the Feast of Trinity to Advent, except in Feasts, and in the Octave of the Blessed Mary, and in the Feast of the Relics, and of All Saints'. Quite obviously, many and varied settings were desirable.[6]

[1] British Museum Add. Ms. 29996, f. 11. Printed in Pfatteicher, *John Redford*, p. 33.
[2] *The Mulliner Book*, p. 43.
[3] *A Plain and Easy Introduction* (ed. Harman), p. 177.
[4] Two settings by Redford (found only in the Mulliner Ms.) are printed in *The Mulliner Book*, pp. 32, 33.
[5] *idem*, p. 44.
[6] Typical examples are printed in Pfatteicher, *op. cit.*, and *The Mulliner Book*.

The Role played by Instruments

Te Deum, the hymn of St. Ambrose and St. Augustine, is always set out in alternating fashion, as are the shorter and more truly metrical hymns. When Henry VII
visited York in 1486 the hymn was sung in the Minster in this way, and the organ
may well have taken part,[1] as it certainly did in the Chapel Royal when celebrations
were ordered (in November 1554) for the reconciliation between England and the
Church of Rome. One of the earliest settings is by Avery Burton, a member of the
Chapel Royal in the early years of Henry VIII's reign, and it is worthy of note that
he makes considerable use of ligatures in his organ verses. These notes bound together
'in ligature' are more often found in vocal than in instrumental music, though there
is a distinct possibility that their continued use was due in some measure to a desire
on the part of the organists to bring out finer points of phrasing. John Redford and
William Blitheman also set *Te Deum*, and displayed considerable agility in their
handling of brilliant decoration and ornament.[2] A constant striving after variety of
mood and texture is shown by the frequent employment of passages in 'proportion',
or what would now be called 6/8 or 9/8 time. In addition to this, the position of the

cantus firmus was subject to change just as much as the number of parts, so that
in performance the organ verses appear to possess an almost kaleidoscopic range of
colour and expression.

Only one example of a Magnificat for organ and plainsong has come down to us,
though this canticle must often have been set by organists. No composer's name is
given, though stylistic links (including a predilection for *alla zoppa* rhythms) suggest
Avery Burton, whose *Te Deum* it immediately follows in the manuscript source. The
piece is simply called 'The viij tune in C fa ut', and is accordingly based on the fabur

[1] Leland, *Collectanea*, IV, p. 191. At the christening of Prince Arthur (also in 1486) *Veni creator* and
Te Deum were sung with organs (*Somers Collection of Tracts*, I, p. 23).
[2] Printed in Pfatteicher, *op. cit.*, and *The Mulliner Book*, p. 55.

den of the eighth tone, transposed to C. The next work in this same manuscript is also unique though far more important. It is the only surviving complete example of an English organ Mass, a form which appears to have originated either in Italy or Germany, and was subsequently much developed in France. The composer is Philip ap Rhys, a Welsh organist who came to London and held posts at various city churches before his appointment to St. Paul's Cathedral. Rhys has set the whole of the Ordinary of the Mass, with the exception of the *Credo* (although there are indications that he intended to compose music for this, too) and he has also included an Offertory which tells us that the work was composed for the feast of the Holy Trinity.[1] The Mass begins with a troped Kyrie *Deus creator omnium*, in which the organist supplies music for the first, third, fifth, seventh, and ninth invocations. *Gloria in excelsis* is likewise set in alternation, though the scheme by which the verses are distributed is quite different from that of any continental organ Mass of the time. The Offertory is an extensive yet carefully-wrought setting of *Benedictus sit Deus Pater*, which is proper to the feast. *Sanctus, Benedictus* and *Agnus Dei* show numerous Tudor characteristics in the matter of style and technique: there is a distinct liking for clear but slightly ascetic counterpoint in two or three parts, coupled with a fondness for melodic sequences and lingering cadences which so frequently find their vocal counterpart in the Henrician and Elizabethan motet.[2]

The only other comparable setting of a large-scale liturgical canvas is by Thomas Preston, whose organ music for the Proper of the Mass on Easter Sunday is the only English example of its kind now extant. Introit (*Resurrexi*), Gradual (*Haec dies*), Alleluia with its verses *Pascha nostrum* and *Epulemur*, and Sequence (*Fulgens praeclara*)

Ex.27   PRESTON: FULGENS PRAECLARA

[Patris]

are all based on the plainsongs or on the faburden.[3] Preston, like Blitheman, was a brilliant player, and there is ample evidence of his resourceful technique in this

---

[1] When Henry VIII and Francis I met in 1520 at the Field of the Cloth of Gold, the English and French chapels alternately sang and played on the organs 'la grant messe *in pontificalibus* qui fut *de trinitate*'. But the name of the composer is not mentioned. See *Lordonnance et ordre du tournoy ioustes et combats . . .* (1520).

[2] The complete Mass is printed in *Altenglische Orgelmusik*, p. 24.

[3] For further details see Stevens, *Further Light on Fulgens Praeclara*, in *Journal of the American Musicological Society*, IX (1956), p. 1.

group of liturgical pieces for Easter. He was a prolific composer of Offertories, and has left eight different yet full-scale versions of *Felix namque*, besides one each of *Reges Tharsis* and *Diffusa est gratia*.

From the middle of the century onwards, organ music became less and less closely bound up with the liturgy. *Felix namque*, a long yet popular plainsong beloved of the organists, was slowly ousted by the rival claims of the 'In nomine' which was sweeping through every musical field of activity from grave consort music to gay and humorous settings of London street cries. The 'In nomine' (often referred to in manuscripts by its correct liturgical title, *Gloria tibi Trinitas*) soon invaded the organ loft, and we find no less than six versions, contained in one and the same manuscript, by William Blitheman.[1] Although, strictly speaking, they do not come under the heading of liturgical organ music, they might well have been used in churches as opening or closing voluntaries. The term 'Voluntary' came into use for the first time at roughly the same date as the vogue of the 'In nomine'. There are two voluntaries, widely different in both size and character, in the Mulliner Book,[2] and two examples by Byrd[3] show that he too followed in the footsteps of Alwood and the elder Farrant. The idea of the voluntary as a free composition without any plainsong basis was fundamentally important, as it heralded the rapid development of fantasia technique which played so great a part in the instrumental music of the seventeenth century. But the organ fantasy remained relatively unimportant in England: for all its freedom from melodic ties, the voluntary, like the fantasy, remained unattractive to keyboard players. Even when organists were so cut off from the Sarum rite as to forget even the names of the melodies, they continued to use them because the plainsong supplied the structural basis which was considered indispensable.

In view of the fluent and idiomatic keyboard style so typical of Byrd at his best, it is perhaps surprising to find that he ventured so rarely into the realms of liturgical organ music. His motets, *Gradualia* and Masses show him to be the kind of stalwart Catholic entirely content to compose music for a liturgy no longer current in his own country, and if he could cheerfully do this, it follows that he might well have written—if only for future use—a corpus of liturgical organ music comparable with that of the early composers. What is most significant is that Byrd's teacher, Thomas Tallis, and his pupil, Thomas Tomkins, have both left a sizeable collection of organ music. Byrd, in between the two, seems not to have thought along the same lines, unless (as has already been hinted) the Commonwealth period saw an end to as many organ books as organs.

Tallis's organ music proves that—apart from the two gigantic settings of *Felix*

[1] *The Mulliner Book*, pp. 67–72.   [2] *idem*, pp. 13, 18.
[3] *Byrd: Complete Works*, XVIII, pp. 44, 45.

namque[1]—vocal polyphony was uppermost in his mind, even when he was actually playing the organ, as undoubtedly he did at Waltham Abbey, Canterbury Cathedral, and the Chapel Royal. Apart from small cadential flourishes and incidental decoration of a discreet nature, there is very little evidence of an organ style even half as idiomatic as that of Redford, Preston and Blitheman. There is, nevertheless, a gracious and contemplative atmosphere about the antiphons and hymn verses which make the listener curious to know more of the composer's keyboard music, and more especially organ music.

Ex.28   TALLIS: EX MORE DOCTI MISTICO

John Bull, who was a pupil of Blitheman, must have written many of his *Gloria tibi Trinitas* settings whilst in England.[2] His other work, which dates from the period of his Antwerp post, falls outside the scope of this book, although it is more truly liturgical than the vigorous and remarkable pieces which appear in the Fitzwilliam Virginal Book, the Tomkins manuscript in the Paris Conservatoire, and other contemporary sources. One piece by Bull, called both 'In nomine' and 'Kyrie eleison' in the Paris manuscript,[3] is in fact neither: it is a setting of a hymn-tune, and thus has no connection with an organ Mass.

The still unchanged double-stave appearance of music right up to the time of Bull and Tomkins, does not preclude the existence of a pedal organ any more than it implies inordinate stretching power in the hands of the organists. There is no doubt that a pedal register of 8 and 4 ft. ranks would have been ideal for the performance of cantus firmi.[4] Assuming a staid and dignified approach to the technique of pedalling the normal progression of a plainsong melody in semibreves or breves would have fitted such an attitude to perfection. Hands would be free to deal with passage-work which was often difficult enough on its own, without the bother of having to hold down a long note throughout a whole bar. But it is often noticeable that composers tended towards notational pessimism, and the thought that their works might have to be played on manuals alone, explains why they often take such care to keep the cantus firmus, whenever possible, within the reasonable ambit of one pair of hands.

Much organ music by Thomas Tomkins, like that of Bull, belongs to the post-

[1] For collated versions see *Thomas Tallis: Complete Keyboard Works* (Hinrichsen-Peters), pp. 10, 20.
[2] See *Musica Britannica*, XIV.   [3] Bibliothèque du Conservatoire, Rés. 1122.
[4] See B. J. Maslen's *The Earliest English Organ Pedals* (*Musical Times*, Sept. 1960).

Elizabethan age;[1] but it has its roots in the early school in more than one sense. Tomkins was a conservative in that he continued to use and exploit the forms known to the Henrician organists, and also to use—almost in copy-book fashion—the priceless manuscripts which had somehow been preserved from the orgy of reform and destruction. His comments, mostly marginal but none the less perspicacious, show him to be a true connoisseur and a fine musician. He knew how to sort out the good from the indifferent, and he corrected orthographical faults with the skill of an editor whose experience is more than life-long. His works are the final flowering of a great tradition.

[1] Most of Tomkins's organ music is available in *Musica Britannica*, V; but three pieces not included in this volume are published by Hinrichsen-Peters. For a critical and historical discussion see Stevens, *Thomas Tomkins, 1572–1656*.

VI

Epilogue

In the *Resolves*, published in 1628, of Owen Feltham, there is a chapter about the nature and effects of music—a conventional chapter, for the most part, with all the accustomed allusions to musical practitioners both classical and mythological. One passage, however, shows that Feltham, in company with other literary men of his time, was not unwilling to make brief reference to his own experience of music: '. . . I think hee hath not a *minde* well tempered, whose zeal is not inflamed by a *heavenly Anthem*. So that indeed *Musicke* is *good*, or *bad*, as the end to which it tendeth.'

The history of Tudor church music shows us that its chief protagonists adopted an attitude which was largely consistent in its idealism and its principal aims. Music, for them, was no proselytizing vehicle, no inflamer of zeal for or against reform. It was an art whose function was to adorn and beautify the ceremonial of the church. Its character, as distinct from its style (which as we have seen, varied considerably within certain limits) embodied to the highest degree those features of repose and reverence without which no liturgical composition is truly complete. Above all, it must be remembered that music of this kind refuses to give up its secrets to those who are content merely to regard its physical aspect, whether in choirbooks, partbooks, or modern scores. It must be heard in conditions which are not only as nearly ideal as possible, but which reproduce exactly the liturgical framework—the *raison d'être* of the original composition.

Feltham's 'heavenly Anthem' reached his ears through no ancillary medium of disc or radio, nor was it read in the silence of his study or reduced to comfortable dimensions by the sound of his clavichord. It was heard in some spacious cathedral or abbey, where sympathetic resonance minimized the faults and exaggerated the virtues of the performance as well as of the composition itself. In other words, the anthem became heavenly through its *milieu* rather than through any intrinsic power

76

of its own, although a composer was naturally bound to present his ideas in such a way that the uplifting, as it were, of his musical offering caused no grave difficulties in execution and involved no unseemly display of vain or earth-bound talents.

As soon as extraneous elements appeared, whether personal or theatrical, attention was drawn from the service of the church to the surface of the music—to all those immediately apparent tricks of harmony, melody, and ornament which flatter and titillate the average ear. Such tricks were commonplaces of church music in England during the eighteenth and nineteenth centuries, and their pernicious influence can still be heard in churches and cathedrals today. Music written for the glorification of choir and organist cannot be other than 'bad, as the end to which it tendeth'. Neglect in avoiding the obvious has often led to the downright banal, so that a canticle intended for choir use, has (through its over-use and its inherent weakness) become ripe for congregational performance. Fortunately participation of this kind is out of the question as far as the Tudor repertory is concerned, except of course in psalms and hymn melodies intended for congregational use.

There is urgent need not only for a complete and integrated study of the entire corpus of Tudor church music, but for an increased knowledge of its treasures in those places where it would undoubtedly achieve the greatest good. There is no lack of variety in its wide span and its catholic embrace of forms and styles; in range alone it links the traditions of the Middle Ages with the new outlook of the baroque era. Without it the history, as well as the musical history, of England would be incalculably the poorer.

Selected Bibliography

Andrews, H. K. 'Printed Sources of William Byrd's "Psalmes, Sonets, and Songs",' *Music & Letters,* xliv, 1963.

Baillie, Hugh. 'A London Church in Early Tudor Times,' *Music & Letters,* xxxvi, 1955.

'A London Gild of Musicians, 1460–1530,' *Proceedings of the Royal Musical Association,* 83rd Session, 1956–7.

'Nicholas Ludford (*c.*1485–*c.*1557),' *Musical Quarterly,* xliv, 1958.

'Squares,' *Acta Musicologica,* xxxii, 1960.

Baillie, H. and Oboussier, P. 'The York Masses,' *Music & Letters,* xxxv, 1954.

Beer, R. 'Byrd's Ornaments,' *Music & Letters,* xxxii, 1951.

Bergsagel, John. 'The Date and Provenance of the Forrest-Heyther Collection of Tudor Masses,' *Music & Letters,* xliv, 1963.

'An Introduction to Ludford,' *Musica Disciplina,* xiv, 1960.

'On the Performance of Ludford's Alternatim Masses,' *Musica Disciplina,* xvi, 1962.

Besseler, Heinrich. 'Das Ergebnis der Diskussion über "Fauxbourdon".' *Acta Musicologica,* xxix, 1957.

Bossewell, John. *Workes of Armorie, Devyded into Three Bookes, Entitled, The Concordes of Armorie The Armorie of Honour, and Coates and Creastes,* 1572.

Boyce, William. *Cathedral Music,* 1760–78.

Boyd, M. C. *Elizabethan Music and Music Criticism,* 1940, 1964.

Brennecke, Ernest. *John Milton the Elder and his Music,* 1938.

Breviarium ad Usum Sarum, ed. F. Proctor and C. Wordsworth, 1879–86.

Bruce, F. F. *The English Bible. A History of Translations,* 1961.

Burney, Charles. *A General History of Music* (1776–89), 1957 reprint of 1935 edition, ed. Frank Mercer.

Butler, Charles. *The Principles of Musick,* 1636.

Calendar of State Papers and Manuscripts Relating to English Affairs . . . in the Archives and Collections of Venice . . ., 1864.

Carver, Robert. *Collected Works* (*Corpus Mensurabilis Musicae,* xvi), ed. Denis Stevens, 1959.

Case, John. *The Praise of Musicke,* 1586.

Chambers, J. D. *Divine Worship in England in the Thirteenth and Fourteenth Centuries,* 1877.

Charles, Sidney Robinson. 'The Provenance and Date of the Pepys Ms 1236,' *Musica Disciplina,* xvi, 1962.

Collins, H. B. 'Byrd's Latin Church Music: For Practical Use in the Roman Liturgy,' *Music & Letters,* iv, 1923.

'John Taverner's Masses,' *Music & Letters,* v, 1924.

'John Taverner—Part II,' *Music & Letters*, vi, 1925.

'Thomas Tallis,' *Music & Letters*, x, 1929.

Dart, Thurston. 'Cambrian Eupompus,' *The Listener*, no. 1359, 1955.

Davey, Henry. *History of English Music*, 1895.

Ellinwood, Leonard. 'Tallis' Tunes and Tudor Psalmody,' *Musica Disciplina*, ii, 1948.

Farmer, H. G. *A History of Music in Scotland*, 1947.

Fellowes, E. H. *English Cathedral Music from Edward VI to Edward VII*, revised 3rd edition, 1964.

    The Office of the Holy Communion as set by John Merbecke, 1949.

    Orlando Gibbons and his Family, 1951.

    William Byrd, 1948.

Flood, W. H. Grattan. *Early Tudor Composers*, 1925.

    'The English Chapel Royal Under Henry V and Henry VI,' *Sammelbände der Internationalen Musikgesellschaft*, x, 1908–9.

Frere, W. H. 'Edwardine Vernacular Services Before the First Prayer Book,' *Alcuin Club Collections*, xxxv, 1940.

Hannas, Ruth. 'Concerning Deletions in the Polyphonic Mass Credo,' *Journal of the American Musicological Society*, v, 1952.

Harrison, Frank Llewellyn. 'An English "Caput",' *Music & Letters*, xxxiii, 1952.

    'The Eton Choirbook,' *Annales Musicologiques*, i, 1953.

    'Faburden in Practice,' *Musica Disciplina*, xvi, 1962.

    'Music for the Sarum Rite (Pepys MS. 1236),' *Annales Musicologiques*, vi, 1958–63.

    Music in Medieval Britain, 1958.

Hawkins, John. *A General History of the Science and Practice of Music*, 1963 reprint of the 1853 Novello edition.

Hendrie, Gerald. 'The Keyboard Music of Orlando Gibbons (1583–1625),' *Proceedings of the Royal Musical Association* 89th Session, 1962–3.

Hughes, Dom Anselm. 'Background to the Roy Henry Music: An Essay in Reconstruction,' *Musical Quarterly*, xxvii, 1941.

    Catalogue of the Musical Manuscripts at Peterhouse, Cambridge, 1953.

    'An Introduction to Fayrfax,' *Musica Disciplina*, vi, 1952.

    Medieval Polyphony in the Bodleian Library, 1951.

    'Sixteenth Century Service Music,' *Music & Letters*, v, 1924.

Hughes-Hughes, Augustus. *Catalogue of Manuscript Music in the British Museum*, 1906–9.

Izon, John. 'Italian Musicians at the Tudor Court,' *Musical Quarterly*, xliv, 1958.

Jackman, James. 'Liturgical Aspects of Byrd's Gradualia,' *Musical Quarterly*, xlix, 1963.

Jebb, J. *The Choral Responses and Litanies of the United Church of England and Ireland*, 1847.

Kenney, Sylvia. '"English Discant" and Discant in England,' *Musical Quarterly*, xlv, 1957.

    'Origins and Chronology of the Brussels Manuscript 5557 in the Bibliothèque Royale de Belgique,' *Revue Belge de Musicologie*, vi, 1952.

Kerman, Joseph. 'On William Byrd's "Emendemus in Melius",' *Musical Quarterly*, xlix, 1963.

    'Byrd's Motets: Chronology and Canon,' *Journal of the American Musicological Society*, xiv, 1961.

    'The Elizabethan Motet,' *Studies in the Renaissance*, ix, 1962.

Lafontaine, H. C. de. *The King's Musick*, 1909.

Leland, John. *De Rebus Britannicis Collectanea*, ed. T. Hearne, 1715.

Selected Bibliography

Letters and Papers, Foreign and Domestic, of the Reign of Henry VIII, ed. J. S. Brewer, 1862–1910.

Lockwood, Lewis. 'A Continental Mass and Motet in a Tudor Manuscript,' *Music & Letters,* xlii, 1961.

Lordonnance et Ordre du Tournoy Ioustes et Combats . . .' 1520.

Lowinsky, Edward. 'On the Use of Scores by Sixteenth-Century Musicians,' *Journal of the American Musicological Society,* i, 1948.

Mace, Thomas. *Musick's Monument,* 1676.

Maslen, B. J. 'The Earliest English Organ Pedals,' *Musical Times,* ci, 1960.

Morley, Thomas. *A Plaine and Easie Introduction to Practicall Musicke,* ed. R. A. Harman, 1952.

North, Roger. *Roger North on Music,* ed. John Wilson, 1959.

Pattison, Bruce. *Music and Poetry of the English Renaissance,* 1948.

Pfatteicher, C. F. *John Redford,* 1934.

Pilgrim Jack. 'Tallis' "Lamentations" and The English Cadence,' *Music Review,* xx, 1959.

Pine, E. 'Westminster Abbey: Some Early Masters of the Choristers,' *Musical Times,* xciv, 1953.

Powicke, Maurice. *The Reformation in England,* 1961.

The Psalter, or Seven Ordinary Hours of Prayer, ed. J. D. Chambers, 1852.

Pulver, J. *A Biographical Dictionary of Old English Music,* 1927.

Reese, Gustave. *Music in the Renaissance,* 1954, 1959.

'The Origin of the English "In Nomine",' *Journal of the American Musicological Society,* ii, 1949.

Rimbault, E. F. *The Old Cheque Book . . . of the Chapel Royal,* 1872.

Rock, D. *The Church of Our Fathers,* ed. G. W. Hart and W. H. Frere, 1903–4.

Rye, W. B. *England as Seen by Foreigners in the Days of Elizabethan and James the First,* 1865.

Schofield, Bertram. 'The Manuscripts of Tallis's Forty-Part Motet,' *Musical Quarterly,* xxxvii, 1951.

Somers Collection of Scarce and Valuable Tracts, 1809–15.

Stevens, Denis. *The Mulliner Book, A Commentary,* 1952.

'The Background of the "In Nomine",' *Monthly Musical Record,* lxxxiv, no. 60, 1954.

'Further Light on Fulgens Praeclara,' *Journal of the American Musicological Society,* ix, 1956.

'The Manuscript Edinburgh, National Library of Scotland, Adv. Ms. 5.1.15,' *Musica Disciplina,* xiii, 1959.

'Processional Psalms in Faburden,' *Musica Disciplina,* ix, 1955.

Thomas Tomkins: 1572–1656, 1957, 1966.

'A Unique Tudor Organ Mass,' *Musica Disciplina,* vi, 1952.

Stevens, John. *Music and Poetry in the Early Tudor Court,* 1961.

'Rounds and Canons from an Early Tudor Songbook,' *Music & Letters,* xxxii, 1951.

Stow, J. *A Survey of London,* 1599.

Strunk, Oliver. *Source Readings in Music History,* 1950.

Trowell, Brian. 'Faburden and Fauxbourdon,' *Musica Disciplina,* xiii, 1959.

Walker, Ernest. *A History of Music in England,* ed. J. A. Westrup, 1952.

Warren, E. B. 'The Life and Works of Robert Fayrfax,' *Musica Disciplina,* xi, 1957.

'The Masses of Robert Fayrfax,' *Musica Disciplina,* xii, 1958.

Wilkins, D. *Concilia Magnae Britanniae et Hiberniae,* 1737.

Willis, B. *A Survey of the Cathedrals,* 1727–30.

Wood, Anthony à. *Athenae Oxonienses; Fasti Oxonienses,* ed. Bliss, 1813–17.

Woodfill, W. *Musicians in English Society from Elizabeth to Charles I,* 1953.

A List of Available Editions of
Tudor Church Music

This list is purely for practical use. It does not include such scholarly editions as the ten volumes of *Tudor Church Music*, *Early English Church Music*, the *Eton Manuscript* volumes and *Music of Scotland* in the series 'Musica Britannica', nor does it include *The Treasury of English Church Music*, Dr. Fellowes's monumental *Complete Works of William Byrd*, or the individual editions of such composers as Fayrfax and Carver now in progress in the series 'Corpus Mensurabilis Musicae' of the American Institute of Musicology. At the time of going to press, all the items listed below were available separately from the publishers indicated. Every endeavour was made to investigate the stock of music advertised, but if there are omissions or corrections the author will be grateful to receive notice of them. Foreign publications have not been listed as they are sometimes difficult to obtain, but readers may like to know of the editions of Fayrfax published by Summy of Chicago, of Tomkins (Concordia Press, St. Louis), of Tallis (Schirmer, New York City), and of Shepherd and Fayrfax (Möseler-Verlag, Wolfenbüttel).

Many editions of Latin church music are also provided with an English translation of the text; conversely a few compositions originally written for Anglican use have a Latin text added. Spurious items, including music printed with words entirely different from the original text, have been eliminated as far as possible. In the list of services and anthems, *italic type* denotes verse settings. The various publishers, whose lists have proved a great help to the compiler, are designated by the following key:

A Ascherberg, Hopwood & Crew, 16 Mortimer Street, London W.1.
B Stainer & Bell, Lesbourne Road, Reigate, Surrey.
C J. &. W. Chester, 11 Great Marlborough Street, London W.1.
F Bayley & Ferguson, 16 Mortimer Street, London W.1.
H Hinrichsen, 10-12 Baches Street, London N.1.
K S.P.C.K., 69 Great Peter Street, London S.W.1.

Music List

N   Novello, 160 Wardour Street, London W.1.
O   Oxford University Press, 44 Conduit Street, London W.1.
P   P.M.M.S., Faith Press, 7 Tufton Street, London S.W.1.
R   Bosworth, 14 Heddon Street, London W.1.
S   Schott, 48 Great Marlborough Street, London W.1.
W   Joseph Williams, 29 Enford Street, London W.1.
X   Curwen, 24 Berners Street, London W.1.
Y   Cary, 16 Mortimer Street, London W.1.

MASSES

Composer	Title	Voices	House	Remarks
Byrd	Mass for Three Voices	ATB	B,C	B has an edition of each of
	Mass for Four Voices	SATB	B,C	Byrd's Masses arranged for
	Mass for Five Voices	SATTB	B,C,X	Anglican use.
Hake	Kyrie	SSAT	B	
Marbecke	Benedictus (Per arma justicie)	SATTB	B	
Okeland	Kyrie	SSAT	B,C	
Packe	Kyrie, Rex summe	STB	C	
Shepherd	Playnsong Mass for a Mene	ATTB	C	
	The French Mass	SATB	C	
Taverner	Kyrie Leroy	SATB	O	
	Mass, The Westorn Wynde	SATB	B,C	
	Mass, Gloria tibi Trinitas	SAATB	B	

SERVICES

Composer	Title	Voices	House	Remarks
Batten	*Fourth Service*			
	Magnificat and Nunc Dimittis	SSATB	O	
	Communion Service	SAATB	O	
	Magnificat and Nunc Dimittis	AATB	O	
Bevin	Magnificat and Nunc Dimittis	SAATB	A	
Byrd	Short Service	SSAATTB	O	Morning and Evening can-
	Magnificat and Nunc Dimittis	SAATB	N	ticles available separately
	Great Service	SSAATTBB	O	Evening canticles available
	Second Service			separately
	Magnificat and Nunc Dimittis	SSAATB	O	
	Third Service			
	Magnificat and Nunc Dimittis	SAATB	O	
	Preces, Responses and Litany	SATB	O	
Causton	Te Deum	SATB	N	
	Magnificat and Munc Dimittis	SATB	N,O	
Farmer	The Lord's Prayer	SATB	O	metrical (Este's *Psalter*)

Farrant, R.	Short Service			
	Magnificat and Nunc Dimittis	SATB	N,O	
Gibbons	First Preces	SAATB	O	with Barnard's Responses.
	Short Service (First)	SATB	N,O	
	Second Service			
	Magnificat and Nunc Dimittis	SSAATTBB	N,O	
Hooper	Second Service			
	Magnificat and Nunc Dimittis	SAATB	O	
	Third Service			
	Magnificat and Nunc Dimittis	SSAATBB	O	
Hunt	Morning and Evening Service	SATB	O	
Loosemore	Litany	SATB	N	
Morley	*First Service*			
	Magnificat and Nunc Dimittis	SSAAATB	O	
	Second Service			
	Magnificat and Nunc Dimittis	SAATB	B	
	Short Service			
	Magnificat and Nunc Dimittis	SATB	O	
Mundy, W.	Magnificat and Nunc Dimittis	SATB	N	
Patrick	Te Deum	SATB	O	
	Magnificat and Nunc Dimittis	SATB	O	
Shepherd	First Service			
	Magnificat and Nunc Dimittis	AATTTBB	O	
Stone	The Lord's Prayer	SATB	K,N	
Tallis	Morning and Evening Service	SATB	F,N,O	N has music for Holy Communion; O gives Mag. and N.D. only.
	Te Deum	SAATB	O	
	Preces, Responses and Litany	SATB	N,O	
Tomkins	First Service			
	Magnificat and Nunc Dimittis	SATB	N	
	Second Service			
	Magnificat and Nunc Dimittis	SATB	O	
	Third Service			
	Magnificat and Nunc Dimittis	SSAATTBB	O	
	Fifth Service			
	Magnificat and Nunc Dimittis	SSAATTBB	O	
Tye	Magnificat and Nunc Dimittis	SATB	N,O	(also attr. to Parsley)
Ward	Magnificat and Nunc Dimittis	SSAATTBB	N,O	
Weelkes	Morning and Evening Service	SATB	B	
	Magnificat and Nunc Dimittis	SSAATB	O	
	Magnificat and Nunc Dimittis	SSATBB	B	("for trebles")
Byrd, Morley, Smith, Tomkins:				
	Preces and Responses		O	

Music List

MAGNIFICATS

Fayrfax	Regali Magnificat	SATTB	B	(two editions available)
Kendall	Dartmouth Magnificat	STBB	B	

MOTETS

anon	O bone Jesu	TTBB	C	Name of Jesus
Blitheman	In pace	SATB	N	Compline
Bramston	Recordare, Domine	TTBB	N	
Browne	O Maria salvatoris mater	SSATTTBB	P	B.V.M.
	Stabat iuxta Christi crucem	TTBBBB	P	B.V.M. (Holy Week)
	Stabat mater	SATTBB	P,B	B.V.M. (Holy Week)
Byrd	Alleluia, Ascendit Deus	SSATB	B	Ascension
	Alleluia, Cognoverunt discipuli	SATB	N	2nd Sunday after Ezster
	Aspice, Domine	SSAATB	B	
	Assumpta est Maria	SATTB	C	B.V.M. Assumption
	Attollite portas	SSAATB	B	
	Ave Maria	SATBB	C	B.V.M.
	Ave regina	SATB	C	B.V.M.
	Ave verum corpus	SATB	B,O,S	Elevation
	Beata es, Virgo Maria	SATTB	C	B.V.M. (Nativity)
	Beata viscera	SATTB	C	B.V.M. (Nativity)
	Cantate Domino	SSATBB	O	
	Christe qui lux es	SATBB	O	Compline
	Christus resurgens	SATB	C	Easter
	Cibavit eos	SATB	B	Corpus Christi
	Civitas sancti tui	SATTB	C,O	Lent
	Confirma hoc, Deus	SSATB	B,C,N,	Pentecost
	Dies sanctificatus	SATB	N	Nativity
	Ego sum panis vivus	SATB	C	Corpus Christi
	Emendemus in melius	SATTB	B	Respond, Ash Wednesday
	Exsurge, quare obdormis Domine	SATTB	O	Sexagesima
	Felix es, sacra Virgo	SATTB	B	B.V.M. (Nativity)
	Haec dies	SSATTB	N,O	Easter
	Hodie beata Virgo	SAATB	N	Purification
	Justorum animae	SSATB	B,N	All Saints
	Laetentur coeli	SATBB	N,O	Nativity
	Laudibus in sanctis	SSATB	B	Verse paraphrase of Ps. 150
	Libera me, Domine et pone	SATTB	B	Respond
	Lumen ad revelationem	SSATB	N	Purification
	Miserere mei	SATBB	O	
	Non vos relinquam orphanos	SSATB	B,C	Pentecost
	O lux beata Trinitas	SSAATB	B	Vespers
	O magnum mysterium	SATB	C,X	Nativity
	O quam gloriosum	SSATB	O	All Saints

Byrd	O quam suavis	SATB	C,N	Corpus Christi	
	O Rex gloriae	SSATB	C	Ascension	
	O sacrum convivium	SATB	C,N	Corpus Christi	
	Oculi omnium	SATB	B	Corpus Christi	
	Peccantem me quotidie	SATTB	B	Office for the Dead	
	Psallite Domino	SSATB	B	Ascension	
	Rorate coeli	SAATB	O	B.V.M. (Masses on Satur-days during Advent)	
	Sacerdotes Domini	SATB	B,O	Corpus Christi	
	Salve regina	SATB	B	B.V.M.	
	Salve regina	SATB	C	B.V.M. (Gradualia)	
	Salve sancta parens	SATBB	C	B.V.M. (Nativity)	
	Senex puerum portabat	SATB	C,N	Purification	
	Senex puerum portabat	SSATB	B	Purification	
	Siderum rector	SSATB	B		
	Surge illuminare	SATB	N	Epiphany	
	Te deprecor	SSATTB	B		
	Terra tremuit	SSATB	N	Easter	
	Tu es pastor ovium	SSATBB	C	SS. Peter and Paul	
	Tu es Petrus	SSATTB	C	SS. Peter and Paul	
	Tui sunt coeli	SATB	N	Nativity	
	Veni Sancte Spiritus	SSATB	B	Pentecost	
	Venite comedite	SATB	Y		
	Victimae Paschali	SSATB	O	Easter	
Cooper	Gloria in excelsis	SSSA	C	Nativity	
Cornysh	Ave Maria	ATTB	B		
	Gaude Virgo	TTBB	B		
Dering	Ave verum corpus	SATTB	S	Elevation	
	Factum est silentium	SSATTB	R	St. Michael	
	Gaudent in caelis	SS	S		
	Gloria Patri	SSA	O		
	Jesu dulcedo cordium	SATTB	R		
	Jesu dulcis memoria	SATTB	R		
	Jesu summa benignitas	SATTB	C	Name of Jesus	
	O bone Jesu	TT	S	Name of Jesus	
	O bone Jesu	SATTB	R	Name of Jesus	
	O vos omnes	SSATTB	R	Holy Saturday	
	Quem vidistis pastores	SSATTB	C,N,R,	Nativity	
	Vox in Rama	SATTB	R		
Fayrfax	Salve regina	SATTB	B	B.V.M.	
Hacomplaynt:	Salve regina	SATTB	B	B.V.M.	
Henry VIII	Quam pulchra es	SSA (or TTB)	B		

85

Music List

Johnson	Dum transisset Sabbatum	SATB	C	Easter
Kellyk	Gaude flore virginali	SATTBB	P	B.V.M.
Kirbye	Vox in Rama	SSATTB	B	Innocents
Lupo	Miserere mei, Domine	SSATB	O	
	O vos omnes	SATTB	C	Holy Saturday
	Salva nos Domine	SSATB	O	
Marbeck	Domine Jesu Christe	SATT	B	
Morley	Agnus Dei	SATB	B,N	
	De profundis clamavi	SSAATB	B,O	
	Domine, Dominus noster	SAATB	B	9th Sunday after Pentecost
	Domine fac mecum	SATB	B,N	
	Domine, non est exaltatum cor	SAATB	B	
	Eheu! sustulerunt Dominum	SATB	B,N	
	Laboravi in gemitu meo	SSAATB	B,O	
	O amica mea	SSATB	B	
Phillips	Alma redemptoris mater	SSATB	C	B.V.M.
	Ascendit Deus	SSATB	O	Ascension
	Ave regina	SSATB	C	B.V.M.
	Ave verum corpus	SSATB	Y	Elevation
	Cantantibus organis	SSATB	N	St. Cecilia
	Ego sum panis vivus	SSATB	W	
	Elegi abjectus esse	SSATB	C	
	Gaudent in coelis	SSATB	N	Common of Martyrs
	Ne reminiscaris Domine	SSATB	N	Lent
	O beatum et sacrosanctum dies	SSATB	C	Nativity
	O crux splendidior	SSATB	S	
	O virum mirabilem	SSATB	C	
	Regina coeli	SSATB	C	B.V.M.
	Surgens Jesus	SSATB	N	3rd Sunday after Easter
	Tibi laus	SSATB	C	Trinity
	Viae Syon lugent	SSATB	N	
Shepherd	Alleluia, Confitemini Domino	TTBB	N	Holy Saturday
	Haec dies	SATTBB	C	Easter
Tallis	Audivi vocem	SATB	O	All Saints
	Dum transisset Sabbatum	SATTB	C	Easter
	Gloria Patri	SATB	N	
	In jejunio et fletu	SATBB	C	Lent
	In manus tuas	SATBB	B	Compline
	Laudate Dominum	SAATB	C	
	O nata lux	SATTB	O	Transfiguration
	O sacrum convivium	SAATB	B	Corpus Christi
	O salutaris hostia	SATTB	C	Corpus Christi
	Salvator mundi (i)	SATTB	O	Holy Cross
	Salvator mundi (ii)	SATBB	C	Holy Cross

Music List

Tallis	Spem in alium	8 choirs of SATBB	O	
	Te lucis ante terminum	SATBB	N	Compline
Taverner	Christe Jesu, pastor bone	SSATB	O	Henry VIII
	Dum transisset Sabbatum	SATBB	B	Easter
	Mater Christi	SATBB	B	B.V.M.
Tayler	Christus resurgens	SATTB	C	Easter
Tye	Omnes gentes plaudite	SATBB	C	
	Rubum quem viderat Moyses	SATBB	C	Circumcision
White	Libera me, Domine	SATB	N	Office for the Dead
	Precamur sancte Domine	SATBB	C	(Verses 2, 4, 6 of *Christe qui lux es;* Compline)
Wright	Nesciens mater	TTBB	C	B.V.M.

VARIA

Byrd	St. John Passion	ATB	B	Good Friday
Davy	St. Matthew Passion	SATB	B	Palm Sunday
Tallis	Lamentations	SATTB	N,O	Holy Week
White	Lamentations	SATTB	B	Holy Week

ANTHEMS

Alison	Behold now praise the Lord	SSATB	B	
	O Lord, bow down Thine ear	SATTB	B	
	The sacred choir of angels	SATBB	B	
Amner	A stranger here	SSAATB	B	
	Away with weak complainings	SAT	X	
	Come, let's rejoice	SSTB	X	
	Love we in one consenting	SST	O	
	My Lord is hence removed and laid	SSATTB	B	
	O ye little flock	SSAATB	O	Nativity
	Sweet are the thoughts	SATB	B	
	The heavens stood all amazed	SSATB	B	
	Thus sings the heavenly choir	SSATB	B	
anon	O Lord, the Maker of all thing	SATB	O	from the Wanley MSS
	This is the day	SATB	O	? Christopher Tye
Batten	Christ our paschal Lamb	AATB	A	
	Deliver us, O Lord	SATB	O	
	Haste Thee, O God	SATB	O	Lent
	Hear my prayer, O Lord	SATB	S	
	Hear my prayer, O God	SAATB	O	
	Lord, we beseech Thee	SATB	N,O	Lent
	O clap your hands together	SSAATTBB	S	
	O praise the Lord	SATB	O	
	O Lord, Thou hast searched me out	SATB	S	
	O sing joyfully	SATB	O	

Batten	*Out of the deep*	SATB	S	
	We beseech thee, Almighty God	SAATB	S	Lent
	When the Lord turned again	SATB	O	
Bevin	Lord who shall dwell	SAB	O	
Bull	*Almighty God, by the leading of a star*	SATB	O	Epiphany
	Attend unto my tears	SATB	B	
	In the departure of the Lord	SATB	B	Holy Saturday
	O Lord, turn not away Thy face	SATBB	B	
Byrd	*An earthly tree*	SSAT	B	Nativity
	Arise, O Lord, into Thy rest	SSTBB	B	
	Attend mine humble prayer	SAT	B	also for ATB
	Be unto me, O Lord, a tower	SATB	N	
	Blessed is he that fears the Lord	SSABB	B	
	Bow thine ear	SATTB	N,O,X	(Civitas sancti tui)
	Christ rising again	SSTTTB	B	Easter
	Come, help, O God	SSATB	N	
	Come let us rejoice	SSAT	B	
	From depth of sin	SAT	B	also for ATB
	From Virgin's womb	TTBB	B	Nativity
	Have mercy upon me	SSATTB	B	
	Help, Lord, for wasted are those men	SSTBB	B	
	How shall a young man?	SSATB	B	
	I have been young	SSA	B	
	I laid me down to rest	SSATB	N	
	If that a sinner's sighs	SSATB	B	
	Look down, O Lord	SATB	N	
	Lord, hear my prayer	SAT	B	also for ATB
	Lord, in Thy rage	SAT	B,S	also for ATB
	Lord, in Thy wrath	SAB	B	also for ATB
	Lord, in Thy wrath	SSATB	B	
	Make ye joy to God	SSTTB	B	
	Mine eyes with fervency	SATTB	B	
	My soul oppressed with care	SSATB	B	
	O God, give ear	SAATB	B	
	O God that guides the cheerful sun	SSATBB	B	
	O God which art most merciful	SAT	B	also for ATB
	O Lord, how long wilt Thou forget?	SAATB	B	
	O Lord, make Thy servant Elizabeth	SAATB	O	Queen Elizabeth I
	O Lord, my God	STTB	B	
	O Lord, turn Thy wrath	SATBB	F	
	O Lord, who in Thy sacred tent	SSABB	B	
	O praise the Lord ye Saints above	SSATB	B	(also attr. to Coperario)

Byrd	Praise the Lord, all ye Gentiles	SSATBB	B	
	Prevent us, O Lord	SAATB	O	(also O, for SATB)
	Prostrate, O Lord, I lie	SATBB	B	
	Right blest are they	SAT	B	also for ATB
	Sing joyfully	SSAATB	B,X	
	Sing we merrily	SSSAT	B	
	Sing ye to our Lord	SSA	B	
	Teach me, O Lord	SSATB	O	
	This day Christ was born	SSAATB	B	Nativity
	Turn our captivity, O Lord	SSTTBB	B	
	Unto the hills	SSTTBB	B	
Causton	Rejoice in the Lord alway	AATB	A	Advent
Dowland	Come, Holy Ghost	SATB	F,N	
	An heart that's broken	SATB	N	
	Thou mighty God	SATB	B	
	When sin sore wounding	SATB	B	
East	When David heard	SSATBB	S	
	When Israel came out of Egypt	SSATB	O	
Farrant	Call to remembrance	SATB	N,O,X	Lent
	Hide not Thou Thy face	SATB	F,N,O	Lent
	Lord, for Thy tender mercy's sake	SATB	F,N	(also attr. to Hilton)
Ferrabosco	In Thee, O Lord	SSSS	B	
Ford	Almighty God	SATB	N,O	
Gibbons, E.	Awake and arise	SSA	A	
Gibbons	Almighty and everlasting God	SATB	N,O	Epiphany
	Almighty God who by Thy Son	SAATBB	N,O	Ember Days
	Deliver us, O Lord	SATB	N	
	Glorious and powerful God	SAATB	N	Whitsun
	Great King of Gods	SAATB	B	King James
	Hosanna to the Son of David	SSAATTB	N,O	Palm Sunday
	If ye be risen again	SSATB	N	Easter
	Lift up your heads	SSAATB	N,O	
	O clap your hands	SSAATTBB	N,O	Ascension
	O God, the King of glory	SAATB	O	Ascension
	O Lord, I lift my heart	AATTB	N	
	O Lord, in Thy wrath	SSAATB	O	Lent
	O Lord, increase my faith	SATB	N	(probably by H. Loosemore)
	See, the Word is incarnate	SSAATB	B	Easter
	This is the record of John	SAATB	N,O	St. John Baptist
	Why art thou so heavy O my soul?	SATB	N	(probably by H. Loosemore)
Giles	Almighty Lord and God of Love	SATB	O	
Heardson	Almighty God, we beseech Thee	SATB	A	
Hilton (younger)	*Teach me, O Lord*	SSATB	O	

Hilton	Call to remembrance	SSAATBB	O	
(elder)	Lord, for thy tender mercy's sake	SATB	N,O	(also attr. to Farrant)
Hooper	Behold, it is Christ	SAATB	S	
	Teach me Thy way, O Lord	SATB	O	
Kirbye	O Jesu, look	SAATB	O	
Lupo	O Lord, give ear	SATB	O	
	Hear my prayer	SAATB	O	
	Out of the deep	SAATB	O	
Marbeck	A Virgin and Mother	SAB	B,H,K	
Morley	Nolo morten peccatoris	SATB	N,O	(also B, for ATTB)
	Out of the deep	SAATB	N	(also O, for SATBB)
	Teach me, O Lord	SATB	B	
	Thou knowest, Lord	SATB	A	Burial Service
Mudd	Let Thy merciful ears, O Lord	SATB	O	(attr. to Weelkes)
	O God who hast prepared	SATB	N,O	
Mundy, J.	*Sing joyfully*	SAATB	O	
Mundy, W.	O Lord, the Maker of all thing	SATB	N,O	
Nicholson	O pray for the peace of Jerusalem	SAATB	O	
	When Jesus sat at meat	SSATB	O	St. Mary Magdalene
Parsons	Deliver me from mine enemies	SSAATB	N	
Peerson	Blow out the trumpet	SSATB	S	
	Lord, ever bridle my desires	SSATB	S	
	Man, dream no more	SSATB	S	
	O God, that no time doest despise	SATB	S	
	O God, when Thou went'st	SSATB	S	
	O let me at Thy footstool fall	SSATB	S	
Pilkington	O gracious God	SSATB	B	
	O praise the Lord	SSATTB	B	
Ramsey	*My song shall be alway*	SATB	B	
	God, who as upon this day	SSATB	S	Whitsunday
	Almighty and everlasting God	SSATB	S	Purification
	Sleep, fleshly birth	SSATTB	B	
Redford (?)	Rejoice in the Lord alway	SATB	N,O	Advent
Shepherd	Haste Thee, O God	SATB	O	
	I give you a new commandment	AATB	O,A	
Smith	*I will wash my hands in innocency*	SAATB	B	
Tallis	Blessed be Thy name	SATTB	O	
	Hear the voice and prayer	SATB	N	
	I give you a new commandment	ATTB	O	
	If ye love me	SATB	F,N	
	O God be merciful	SATB	O	
	O Lord, give Thy Holy Spirit	SATB	A,N,O	Pentecost
	Purge me, O Lord	SATB	F,O	
	This is my commandment	SSATB	A,O	Holy Week

Tomkins	Almighty and everlasting God	SATB	H	Ash Wednesday
	Almighty God, the fountain of all wisdom	SAATB	S	
	Behold the hour cometh	SSATB	S	
	God, who as at this time	SATB	H	Pentecost
	Great and marvellous	SAATB	O	
	Have mercy upon me	SAB	O	
	I heard a voice from heaven	SATB	N	Burial Service
	My beloved spake	SATB	S	
	My Shepherd is the living Lord	SATB	B	
	O give thanks	ATTB	O	
	O God, wonderful art Thou	SAATB	O	
	O how amiable	ATTB	O	
	O Lord, I have loved	SAATB	H	
	O praise the Lord all ye heathen	3S3A3T3B	O	
	O pray for the peace of Jerusalem	SSTB	O	
	O sing unto the Lord	SSAATBB	S	
	Then David mourned	SSATB	H,S	
	Thou art my King, O God	SAATB	B	
	Turn unto the Lord	SSATTB	B	
	When David heard	SAATB	B	
Tye	I will exalt Thee	SATB	O	
	O God be merciful	SATB	O	
	Praise ye the Lord	SATB	O	
	Sing unto the Lord	SATB	O	
Ward	O let me tread	SATB	O	
Weelkes	All people clap your hands	SAATB	O	
	Alleluia, I heard a voice	SSTBB	O	
	Gloria; Sing my soul	SSAATB	O	
	Hosanna to the Son of David	SSATBB	O	
	Let Thy merciful ears	SATB	O	(probably by Thos. Mudd)
	Lord, to Thee I make my moan	SAATB	O	
	O how amiable	SAATB	O	
	O Jonathan	SSAATB	N,S	
	O Lord, arise into Thy resting place	SSAATBB	O	
	O Lord God Almighty	SAATB	O	Royal Family
	O Lord, grant the King a long life	SSAATBB	O	
	When David heard	SSAATB	N	
White	O how glorious	SAATB	O	
	O praise God	SSAATTBB	H	
	O praise God	SATB	N,O	
Wilson	Behold, now praise the Lord	SATB	A	

A Note on the Music Recorded

Fayrfax: *Sanctus*

This is from the Mass *Tecum principium*, a particularly fine example of a Mass built upon a cantus firmus, in this case the antiphon to the first psalm (*Dixit Dominus*) at Second Vespers on Christmas Day. Fayrfax uses a five-part choir (SATBB) and secures the maximum contrast in playing off a high group of voices against a lower group. The massive sonority of the full choir is reserved for the sections 'Dominus Deus Sabaoth' and 'Hosanna'.

Text: *Sanctus, Sanctus, Sanctus Dominus Deus Sabaoth. Pleni sunt caeli et terra gloria tua. Hosanna in excelsis.*

Holy, Holy, Holy, Lord God of Hosts, heaven and earth are full of Thy glory. Hosanna in the highest.

Robert Stone: *The Lord's Praier*

A simple, yet beautiful four-part setting which was printed in Day's *Certaine Notes* (1560). Apart from one or two words, the text is exactly the same as that of the Prayer Book of 1661.

Blitheman: *In pace in idipsum*

This responsory was sung at Compline from the first Sunday in Lent until Passion Sunday. It illustrates succinctly the basic formula of a part of the liturgy that was often set for alternating solo group and plainsong chorus. Some responsories were quite complex, and the composer had to make allowances in his polyphony for repeats of the latter portion of the responsory. This was usually arranged by placing a clearly recognizable cadence, followed by the *repetenda*, at the point where the join was to be made. The scheme of Blitheman's setting is as follows (S = Soloists, C = Chorus):

S: *In pace*	In peace
C: *in idipsum dormiam et requiescam.*	in the very same I will sleep and take my rest.
S: *Si dedero somnum oculis meis et palpebris meis dormitationem*	If I give sleep to mine eyes, and to mine eyelids slumber
C: *dormiam et requiescam.*	I will sleep and take my rest.
S: *Gloria Patri et Filio et Spiritui Sancto.*	Glory be to the Father, and to the Son, and to the Holy Ghost.
In pace	In peace
C: *in idipsum dormiam et requiescam.*	in the very same I will sleep and take my rest.

Byrd: *O Lord, make Thy servant Elizabeth our Queen*

This is a piece of occasional music, set for six-part choir, and is a prayer for the Queen. It long continued in use in the Chapel Royal, for later sources substitute the names of James and Charles for that of Elizabeth.

Text: O Lord, make Thy servant Elizabeth our Queen to rejoice in Thy strength; give her her heart's desire, and deny not the request of her lips, but prevent her with Thine everlasting blessing, and give her a long life, even for ever and ever. Amen.

The music used for this record has been newly edited from the original sources by Denis Stevens.

Index

Sarum settings of Kyrie, Gloria, etc., are distinguished from Anglican settings by the use of italic type.

Index